ADDITIONAL RESOURCES
AND MATERIALS

Go to www.modernparable.com
to take advantage of online resources on the parables
as well as to purchase additional materials.

INDIVIDUAL DVD'S

STUDY BOOKS

LEADER'S GUIDES

GROUP STUDY DVD BOX SET

DIGITAL DOWNLOADS

MOVIE POSTERS
(FOR USE IN ANNOUNCING THE CLASS)

BOOKS ON THE PARABLES

*Actual posters include space at the bottom
for writing class information.*

CINEMATIC THEOLOGY™

MODERN
PARABLES®

LIVING IN THE KINGDOM OF GOD

VOLUME I

Study Book

Thomas Purifoy, Jr. & Jonathan Rogers, Ph.D.

"What shall we say the kingdom of God is like, or what parable shall we use to describe it?"

MARK 4:30

Book design: Abe Goolsby, Officina Abrahae

ISBN: 0-9798524-1-2 / 978-0-9798524-1-1

Printed in the United States of America.

TABLE OF CONTENTS

Introduction

A New Kind of Study

Modern Parables is a new kind of Bible study. From one perspective, it's a study that uses short films of the parables to teach the Bible.

But from another perspective, it's something unique. *Modern Parables* employs a new method of understanding the Bible through films that explain the biblical text. It uses modern stories that recreate in the viewer the same responses that the original audiences of Jesus' parables might have experienced. In other words, *just watching the films* begins to explain the historical, grammatical, contextual and interpretive elements of Jesus' parables. The films help people grasp the parables at an immediate, gut level. This emotional immediacy enables them to engage the Bible in a powerful and compelling new way.

At its heart, *Modern Parables* uses film to drive people deeper into Scripture. To borrow a phrase from the poet Horace, it seeks "to please and instruct." The films are intended to be both entertaining and educational at the same time.

Most people – churchgoing people, at least – would agree that Jesus' parables are important. Yet, if asked further, most would say that His parables are nice stories intended to teach universal moral lessons. If you understand the moral of the story, you've gotten the parable.

There's a problem with that explanation: it doesn't square with what Jesus Himself said about His parables. Rather than trying to create a set of nice stories for the world, Jesus bluntly said that He taught in parables so that His hearers *wouldn't immediately understand* His teaching (Matt 13:13).

But the problem goes beyond that. When you start looking at His parables, a lot of them aren't nice stories at all: a king destroys an entire city for speaking out against him; a manager cheats his master out of money and is praised by Jesus for it; a fig tree is cursed for not bearing fruit.

When taken at face value, the parables can be confusing and hard to understand. In fact, to get a nice moral out of some of them requires a good bit of twisting. Parables are not simple moral stories that teach a lesson.

So what are parables?

The Bible explains that Jesus had specific purposes for teaching in parables. Matthew tells us that in at least one instance He spoke to the crowd *only* in parables and said nothing without a parable (Matt 13:34). Why is this?

As Jesus said in Mark, "What shall we say the kingdom of God is like, or what parable shall we use to describe it?" (Mk 4:30) It is important to understand that the parables cannot be separated from Jesus' teaching on the Kingdom of God. If detached from His larger teaching ministry, they don't make sense. Rather, the parables are like different lenses used to view different aspects of the Kingdom of God. Jesus Himself often started His parables with, "The Kingdom of God is like..."

To Jesus, parables are comparisons between the natural and spiritual realms that teach His followers different aspects of the Kingdom of God. In this sense, parables are keys to understanding the things Jesus wanted His followers to know about His Kingdom. On the one hand, they are like little instruction manuals explaining what God is like and how He acts, as well as how people in His Kingdom *ought* to live. On the other hand, they describe how people inside or outside the Kingdom *actually do* live.

The reason Jesus spoke in parables was that He knew they were the best method for teaching about the Kingdom He was inaugurating with His life, death, and resurrection.

Closing Thoughts

In the weeks ahead, you'll be studying six different parables. They are:

    Lessons 1 & 2 – *Hidden Treasure* – Matthew 13:44
    Lessons 3 & 4 – *Samaritan* – Luke 10:25-37
    Lessons 5 & 6 – *The Shrewd Manager* – Luke 16:1-9
    Lessons 7 & 8 – *The Widow & Judge* – Luke 18:1-8
    Lessons 9 & 10 – *The Sower* – Matthew 13:1-23
    Lessons 11 & 12 – *Prodigal Sons* – Luke 15:11-32

Each parable is covered in two lessons. The first lesson for each parable is called "Understanding the Parable." In this lesson you'll be watching a film, then doing some basic study on the parable itself. The second lesson for each parable is called "Living the Parable." In this lesson you'll be watching an application video taught by one of six different pastors, then discussing how to apply the teaching of the parable in your day-to-day life.

This volume has been written assuming that you'll <u>read the chapters in this book *after* the corresponding lesson</u>. Of course you don't have to do this, but there are movie spoilers in the book and most people don't like spoilers.

The goal of this class is for you to grow in your understanding of the Kingdom of God as explained through Jesus' parables and to live out the parables' teaching in your daily life. It is our hope that you have an enjoyable time doing it.

Thomas Purifoy, Jr.
Producer, *Modern Parables*

Matthew 13:44

Hidden Treasure

UNDERSTANDING THE PARABLE

> The kingdom of heaven is like treasure hidden in a field. When a man
> found it, he hid it again, and then in his joy went and sold all he had
> and bought that field. MATT 13:44

Introduction

There is a story about a major oil company that drilled some
test wells in a largely agricultural and rural area of Florida in the
1970's. After the results came in, they announced that the wells
were non-productive. The company then had agents go around
inconspicuously and buy up land and oil rights from the farmers for very little money. One farmer, thought to be a bit crazy
because of his eccentric ways, decided there really was oil under
his land and decided to keep his farm and oil rights. He tried to
convince others to do the same, but no one would listen to him.

After the oil company had bought up most of the rights for
pennies on the dollar, they returned to the area and started
extracting barrels upon barrels of oil from the land. The
"crazy" farmer then sold his land and rights for a fortune and
became a millionaire.[1]

Stories about an underdog thinking quickly and making a fortune as a result are exciting to hear. Throughout history and across cultures, there are similar accounts of average people suddenly happening on a priceless find, having to act quickly and cleverly to secure the treasure, then changing their lives forever because of it.

Jesus understood this delight. In telling the parable of the Hidden Treasure, He played on the universal desire to see one's life suddenly transformed into something wonderful.

The Background of Hidden Treasure

The parable of the Hidden Treasure is one of Jesus' shortest parables. Matthew records it for us in chapter 13 along with the other great parables explaining the Kingdom of God (the sower, the wheat and the tares, and the mustard seed, among others).

In providing the historical setting of the parable, Matthew tells us that "Jesus went out of the house and sat by the lake. Such large crowds gathered around him that he got into a boat and sat in it, while all the people stood on the shore." (Matt 13:1-2) Jesus would have been speaking to a crowd made up of some Pharisees (with whom he had argued earlier in the day) as well as many local peasants from the surrounding countryside. All of them had traveled to hear what this new teacher (or rabbi) had to say.

It was not unusual for Jewish rabbis to speak in parables. In fact, the Hebrew prophets and teachers of old had developed this particular form through their unique understanding of the way God had created the world. They recognized that some truths can best be explained in stories.[2] It's not hard to understand why: parables work in the familiar world of the everyday, taking abstract concepts such as loving God and loving one's neighbor, then putting flesh on them. This recognition that there *must* be a relationship between theology and reality is an important aspect of true, Biblical religion.

But if it wasn't unusual to hear rabbis speak in parables, it *was* unusual for a rabbi not to explain exactly what the parable meant after telling it. There were a few exceptions, but Jesus typically didn't explain Himself. In fact, during this particular preaching time, Matthew tells us that He spoke to this crowd only in parables and "did not say anything without using a parable." (Matt 13:34) Jesus' method concerned his disciples, so they asked Him why it was that He spoke to the people in parables (Matt 13:10).

His answer was a bit surprising.

Why Did Jesus Teach in Parables?

As we saw in the Introduction, the central theme of Jesus' teaching ministry was to explain the Kingdom of God. Although His teaching method was one with which His first-century listeners were familiar, there was more to the method than they realized. Jesus knew that the parable form perfectly emphasized what He wanted to teach: that is, how *the spiritual Kingdom of God is pressing into and transforming the natural world of the here and now.*[3]

To Jesus, the Kingdom of God was about how His redemptive action was going to affect the daily, individual lives of His followers both in the present and the future. The parables have that as their central concern.

Yet Jesus understood that spiritual things are often difficult to comprehend. What is the Kingdom really worth? What does it mean to receive God's grace? How does repentance work? What is love? By using the parables as comparisons between the natural and spiritual realms, Jesus was creating a series of doors through which His listeners could step and actually *enter into* a new understanding about His Kingdom. As one writer has put it, the parables are nothing less than "spiritual discoveries" about the way God's creation truly works.[4]

But Jesus' parables had a catch to them.

In answering their question, Jesus explained to His disciples that, "The secret of the kingdom of God has been given to you. But to those on the outside everything is said in parables so that, 'they may be ever seeing but never perceiving, and ever hearing but never understanding; otherwise they might turn and be forgiven!'" (Mark 4:10-12)

In other words, Jesus was saying, 'I'm speaking in parables *so they won't easily understand."*

Why did Jesus want the truth veiled from so many of His hearers? And what was the "secret" He was referring to?

It's important to recognize that Jesus' first-century Jewish audience already had strong opinions about the Kingdom of God. Just as Christians today hold very strong opinions about the second coming of Christ, so too did the first-century Jews about the coming of the Messiah. From their interpretation of the Old Testament, everyone expected a powerful Messiah to come suddenly, wipe out the Roman oppressors, then quickly set up a magnificent, visible kingdom here on earth. Luke reveals this popular mentality when he writes: "[Jesus] went on to tell them a parable, because he was near Jerusalem and the people thought that the kingdom of God was going to appear at once." (Luke 19:11)

The primary problem with this popular interpretation was that it was wrong. In complete disregard of everyone's assumptions and expectations, God sent a suffering servant to establish a spiritual kingdom that would slowly grow to fill "the entire earth." (Dan 2:35) This true kingdom would certainly have physical manifestations – but not those assumed by Jesus' audience.

That was the secret. *Unless one understood that Jesus and His unique ministry were what the parables were talking about, then one could not understand His parables.*[5] The secret that had been revealed to the disciples was Jesus Himself and His unexpected method of redemption. As God prophesied in Isaiah (and was quoted by Paul in Romans), "See, I lay in Zion a stone that causes men to stumble and a rock that makes them fall, and the one who trusts in him will never be put to shame." (Romans 9:33/Isaiah 8:14) Many people of Jesus' day stumbled and fell over what Jesus appeared to be: a gentle man, a humble man, a powerless man. Because so many people rejected Jesus as the Son of God, they were "ever seeing, but never understanding."

This brings us to a final reason why Jesus taught in parables. Parables are the perfect method for sneaking past prejudices and misconceptions concerning the Kingdom of God. By creating a world that listeners willingly entered into, they checked their preconceived notions at the door. Of course, once inside the world, they found themselves interested and often convicted by the actions of the fictional characters. This would make hearers angry and push them to reject Jesus' message entirely (as many Pharisees often did); it would leave people scratching their heads (as many peasants often did); or it would drive people to true change.

In sum, Jesus taught in parables because they:

1   Were familiar to His audience,
2   Could communicate the truth quickly and effectively,
3   Used the relationship between the natural and spiritual realms to make complex ideas easy to understand,
4   Veiled the truth from those who did not recognize His unique ministry, and
5   Created a fictional world that slipped past prejudices and misconceptions concerning the Kingdom of God.

We see all this happening perfectly in the parable of the Hidden Treasure.

Exploring Hidden Treasure

The kingdom of heaven is like treasure hidden in a field. When a man found it, he hid it again, and then in his joy went and sold all he had and bought that field. MATT 13:44

Names of the Kingdom

The kingdom of heaven...

We stated earlier that Jesus used the parables to teach about the Kingdom of God. But Matthew quotes Jesus as saying "kingdom of heaven," not "kingdom of God." There is only one Kingdom, but the gospel writers do not always use the same phrase when referring to it. Matthew primarily uses the phrase "kingdom of heaven" (although he does use "kingdom of God" four times), whereas Mark and Luke always use the phrase "kingdom of God." Why is this?

Since the gospels were all written in Greek, we can be sure that Jesus – who spoke Aramaic – used neither of these phrases exactly. Rather the writers of the gospel were interpreting the Aramaic phrase that Jesus used and translating it into Greek. Matthew was writing to a more Jewish audience who, in accordance with their religious history, avoided using the actual name of God. It was therefore more reverent to say "kingdom of heaven" with "heaven" indirectly referring to God Himself. Since Mark and Luke were writing to predominantly non-Jewish audiences, they used the phrase that would be least confusing. For the sake of simplicity, this study will quote Matthew accurately but will always refer to God's Kingdom as the Kingdom of God.

Comparing the Kingdom

...is like...

Jesus spent a lot of His ministry talking about the Kingdom. But at no time in any of the gospels did He define exactly what He meant by the Kingdom of God. Instead, He just took the well-used phrase and applied new comparisons and teachings to it. He clearly expected His followers to be able to figure out what He was talking about.

We said in the Introduction that parables *are comparisons between the natural and spiritual realms that Jesus uses to teach His followers different aspects of the Kingdom of God.* But how exactly do these comparisons work?

That's not easy to answer. In the only recorded instances when Jesus explained parables to His disciples (just three times), His method of comparison follows the lines of a simple allegory. An allegory is a type of story where the different characters and elements stand for things outside the world of the story. The most famous Christian allegory is John Bunyan's *Pilgrim's Progress,* which includes characters named "Christian," "Mr. Worldly Wiseman," "Mr. Legality" and places named "Hill Difficulty" or "Doubting Castle." Bunyan did not leave much to the imagination to figure out what the characters and places were supposed to represent.

In the three recorded instances, Jesus is just as detailed about the parallels between the parable and the spiritual world. For instance, in explaining the parable of the Tares and the Weeds (Matt 13:24-30) He said, "The one who sowed the good seed is the Son of Man. The field is the world, and the good seed stands for the sons of the kingdom. The weeds are the sons of the evil one, and the enemy who sows them is the devil. The harvest is the end of the age, and the harvesters are angels." (Matt 13:37-39)

This is pretty detailed. It's also straightforward allegory. Does this mean that Jesus used allegory this detailed in all His parables? Again, that's hard to say. There is a long history of allegorical interpretation of the parables stretching back to the earliest centuries of the Christian era. The problem with most of the interpretations is that on many details few people can seem to agree. For thousands of years the church has created complex comparisons that don't always last beyond that period of church history.

What does that mean for us? It's clear that Jesus was making comparisons with the parables and that they were simple comparisons. Keeping comparisons simple usually results in general agreement *and* seems to make better interpretational sense. But how do we find simplicity in stories that are so famously *not* straightforward? Thankfully the Gospel writers were usually straightforward in depicting the context in which Jesus told His parables—*where, to whom, why*. The context frequently yields important clues as to what Jesus meant to communicate.

For instance, the parable of the Prodigal Son was told to a group of tax collectors and sinners together with a group of Pharisees. It makes sense that the points of comparison would be between the younger son as a sinner and the older son as a self-righteous law-abider. Often the gospel writers or Jesus will make hints as to how we should be interpreting the parables. Understanding the context is therefore most valuable to seeing how the comparisons work out.

Of course "getting" the comparison does not mean that we understand the parable. In fact, linking the dots and then stopping there could be one of the worst things we could do. Rather, Jesus wants us to enter into and engage the story itself. In most cases, one of the points of comparison should be to ourselves.

A Question of Value

...treasure hidden in a field.

Today, most people would consider a bank the safest place to store something valuable. But that was not the case two thousand years ago. In the Middle East — where war was normally just over the horizon and invaders as regular as the spring rain — it was necessary to store one's treasures in places that were virtually impossible for others to locate. Even today there's nothing quite as unassuming and (at least before the advent of metal detectors) as inscrutable as a big field.

Josephus, the first-century Jewish historian, tells us in his *Antiquities* that the people of his day often used fields to hide their treasures before invaders arrived. But it was also possible for those same people to be killed in warfare and their secret to die with them. In fact, although it was probably rare, finding treasure in a field would have happened from time to time — at least often enough for Jesus' listeners to nod with understanding at His plot. After all, if the owner in the story didn't know about the treasure (and he would never have sold his property had he known about it), then the land had clearly changed hands a few times before coming into his possession.

But what was this treasure? Jesus didn't say but we can surmise it would have been precious metals and jewels, the things in that day and age that represented the best way to consolidate wealth as well as the easiest to hide. Whatever it was, it was something that the finder knew instantly was of inestimable worth and that he had to have it.

This is the first point of comparison for the parable. As the context of Matthew 13 would show us, Jesus was making a direct comparison between the attributes of the Kingdom and those of a treasure, just as earlier He made exact comparisons between the Kingdom and yeast, a net, a field, etc. Following that comparison through, we can say that the Kingdom is valuable and priceless. But what is even more important is that because the Kingdom is so valuable, *it can transform the lives of those possessing it.*

This is where we pick up our film's main character, Jeff Smith. Jeff is just an average guy going about his business when he stumbles across oil bubbling up from the ground on the property he is showing. Just like the field in the parable, the ugly piece of property appears to be devoid of any special value. It's the kind of property you'd pass by and think in your mind how worthless it appears. Although the original parable does not say the field appeared to be worthless, in that day and age fields were literally everywhere. Yes, they were valuable — but only as valuable as what they could be used for. No field was going to change anyone's life.

That is, unless there was treasure buried under it. And for our point of comparison, there are few things worth more money in our day than large supplies of crude oil. Everyone knows that oil fields have made countless millionaires — and Jeff, though it takes him a moment to figure it out, is not slow to realize what it means to him. In Jesus' day there was a big gap between the rich and the poor. Treasure to a peasant would mean a radical change of lifestyle, a complete transformation into something previously impossible, a new world unexpectedly opening up to him.

But the treasure is not obvious, not there for all to see. In fact, nearly everyone would overlook it. What is Jesus telling us about the Kingdom with this? That it is not out in plain view for all to comprehend? That it could be missed by thousands? That it is somehow invisible? (Luke 17:20) And what does that mean for those not in the Kingdom?

Finders Keepers

When a man found it...

The first-century listener would immediately know the kind of man who spent time in fields. Not being an owner himself, the man was likely a simple laborer who had been hired to work in that field. He would not have been a rich man; rich men didn't work in fields. And it would have been understood by the listeners that he was working since he *uncovers* the treasure. The kind of worker who uncovers things in a field is likely either plowing or digging: tough work by any measure. Moreover, it's work done by a man closer to the bottom of the economic scale.

This is where we find Jeff Smith. He's not a particularly successful real estate agent, but he works hard. He would be considered on the lower side of middle class: he has a family, a mortgage, and a car payment — with one job to support it all. When he's out trying to sell this piece of land, he's not expecting to get rich doing it.

And this is what is so interesting about this parable: it is seemingly accidental that the man stumbles upon the treasure. It almost reveals itself to him — he is doing nothing to look for it other than going about his daily routine.

Again, what is Jesus telling us about the Kingdom? Although it is hidden from many, it somehow reveals itself to certain people in their course of daily life. It appears that the Kingdom presents itself suddenly in front of unsuspecting eyes — and then requires an immediate, life-changing decision.

Quick Thinking

...he hid it again...

Here begins the crux of the parable. The man could potentially do any number of things after finding the treasure: he could tell the owner, he could ignore it, he could leave it uncovered. But he realizes what it means to him and hatches a plan to acquire it for himself. By choosing to hide it, he begins to take action to possess the treasure.

This is what the parable of the Hidden Treasure is all about: when an extraordinary treasure presents itself to someone, *that person must choose to act* to acquire the treasure. Passivity is useless here. According to Jesus, the Kingdom often reveals itself to people unexpectedly in their daily lives. And unless they take immediate action to acquire it for themselves, they cannot have it.

Of course a number of modern readers will think that the man is being unethical. Shouldn't he inform the owner of the field? Yet here again we see an important difference between our culture and theirs: to the first-century Middle-Easterner, shrewdness was equated to wisdom. The man was doing nothing illegal. It was the owner's responsibility to know what was his.

Even more, it is expected that when the Kingdom reveals itself to someone, he will have the wisdom to recognize it and know what to do about it. The Bible consistently teaches that shrewdness is a valuable trait — not shrewdness that is outright deceptive, but a shrewdness that understands how to work a situation to one's advantage. After all, it is Jesus himself who tells us to be "as shrewd as snakes and as innocent as doves." (Matt 10:16) If this seems unusual to us, perhaps it's because we don't truly understand how Jesus wants us to act in the world. In the case of the hidden treasure, He clearly wants us to emulate the man who does everything in his power to lawfully take hold of the treasure in front of him.

The Right Reaction

...then in his joy...

The man's reaction shows us how we should react to the Kingdom. Think of Jeff's bursting elation at realizing what owning the field could mean to him. This joy — an exuberance that overflows boundaries — is what the Kingdom is really about. Most people remember watching Ed McMahon showing up on someone's doorstep and announcing that they just won the Publisher's Clearinghouse Sweepstakes. People would scream, faint, jump up and down, hug Ed — they were bursting with joy at the prospect.

Why?

Because they immediately knew their lives were going to be changed forever. This is the strong dynamic at the heart of the parable that we cannot overlook. Possessing the Kingdom is not like having a priceless ring or watch that we show off with pride. Rather, *possessing the kingdom is about radical life-change. The emotions that accompany it spring from the knowledge that everything is going to be better because of what the Kingdom makes possible.* The joy is not simply about the treasure, but about what the treasure represents: a completely new life.

Selling Everything

...went and sold all he had...

The man continues to act aggressively. It seems as if Jesus is implying that the Kingdom does not sit idly by and wait: rather, it must be taken aggressively and by forceful action. He says as much when He tells us that "forceful men lay hold of it." (Matt 11:12) The Kingdom pushes people to make a decision; yet for those to whom the Kingdom has been revealed, it is an easy choice. In fact, they realize they would be foolish to do anything else.

Selling everything may seem foolhardy on the surface. Jeff runs up against this with his wife and his friends. We are assuming that the family and relations of the man in the parable thought he was crazy, perhaps even after they understood exactly what he was gaining. To those who haven't actually seen the treasure, it might seem very risky.

Please note that the original parable does not go into these details. Rather, they have been added into the film as reflections on the story based on things Jesus tells us in other places about the influences of family and possessions on the decision to pursue the Kingdom. (Luke 9:59-61; Mark 10:29-30)

After all, what is "all he had" a comparison to? In numerous places Jesus tells us that our worldly attachments have to be given up for us to acquire the Kingdom. Furthermore He says that if we do not give them up, they will actually keep us from entering the Kingdom: "How hard it is for the rich to enter the kingdom of God! Indeed, it is easier for a camel to go through the eye of a needle than for a rich man to enter the kingdom of God." (Luke 18:24-25) And "any of you who does not give up everything he has cannot be my disciple." (Luke 14:33)

To press this further, it may superficially appear that the man is sacrificing everything to gain the Kingdom. And in one sense, that is true – but is it really a sacrifice? Or is he merely giving up what little he has to gain so much more? Although it may appear to the outside world that a disciple is giving up everything for a foolish dream, yet the disciple understands that what he is gaining is worth infinitely more than he is giving up.

This is an important point since some commentators debate whether this parable is about the value of the kingdom or the cost of discipleship. In our opinion, these categories do not completely capture the thrust of the parable, which is: *the disciple must take immediate action to sell everything to gain the Kingdom for himself, both in light of its value and in spite of its cost.* It is the <u>action</u> of the man that must be the center of our thinking.

The Kingdom may be of infinite value, and it may cost us all that we have, *but unless we take action to acquire it* then its worth is irrelevant to us. Everything pivots on gaining the Kingdom.

The Buy of a Lifetime

...and bought that field.

Once he has enough money in hand, he immediately moves to close the transaction. After all, until he owns the field the treasure is not his. It is interesting to think that while he knows about the treasure, he does not possess it. Knowledge is not enough for possession. Had Jeff not taken the decisive actions of convincing his wife, of selling everything, and of purchasing the field in spite of the advice of his friends, his life would have remained unchanged.

Everything comes down to the purchase: we acquire the Kingdom by transaction, an act of choosing and taking hold. Without that action the Kingdom will elude us.

Summary

We have seen that the parable of the Hidden Treasure is primarily about the immediate action of the person who finds the Kingdom to gain it for himself, both in light of its value and in spite of its cost. Although it may appear to be an unwise decision from the world's eyes, it is the utmost wisdom to give up what is nearly worthless for something absolutely priceless. Such a situation demands quick thinking and even quicker action on the part of the potential disciple. After all, unless action is taken, it is possible that the treasure might be lost forever.

PARALLELS

ORIGINAL PARABLE	PARABLE FILM
Treasure is riches and wealth in the form of gold, jewels or precious objects.	Treasure is riches and wealth in the form of a large oil reserve.
Treasure is hidden in a field so not easily seen by people passing by.	Oil is underground and hidden so not easily seen by people passing by.
The field is a common, not particularly noteworthy, place.	The old property is a common, not particularly noteworthy, place.
The man was likely a laborer and not wealthy.	Jeff is an unsuccessful real estate agent and not wealthy.

The man is not looking for treasure, and it surprises him to find it.	Jeff is not looking for oil, and it surprises him to find it.
The man hides it again so no one else will find it.	Jeff covers up his tracks so no one else will find it.
The man is joyful over his find because he understands how the treasure could change his life.	Jeff is thrilled over his find because he understands how the oil could change his life.
The man returns to his home to prepare to sell his things.	Jeff returns to his home to prepare to sell his things.
The man sells everything he owns to gather enough money to buy the field.	Jeff sells everything he owns to gather enough money to buy the field.
The man purchases the field.	Jeff purchases the field.

Endnotes

1 As recounted by Andrew Ivestor from stories his uncle told after having lived near that area of Florida.

2 Brad Young, *The Parables: Jewish Tradition and Christian Interpretation* (Hendrickson, 1998), 4.

3 Geerhadus Vos, *The Kingdom and the Church* (Eerdmans, 1958), 45.

4 Geerhardus Vos, *Biblical Theology* (Banner of Truth, 1992), 355. This is what Matthew means when he says Psalm 72:2 was fulfilled in Jesus (Matt 13:35). Jesus understood that there is a direct relationship between the natural and spiritual realms. After all, He created the natural realm and all that is in it. Certain aspects of the world we live in (for instance: sheep, marriage, seeds) were created so that they would mirror certain aspects of the spiritual realm (respectively: believers, the relationship between Christ and the Church, spiritual growth). This is not a coincidence. Jesus knew that He could go to this ready-made set of images and use them to guide his listeners easily through profound - and potentially complex - teachings about God, and man's relationship to Him.

5 Herman Ridderbos, *The Coming of the Kingdom* (P&R, 1962), 123.

LESSON TWO

Hidden Treasure

LIVING THE PARABLE

The kingdom of heaven is like treasure hidden in a field. When a man found it, he hid it again, and then in his joy went and sold all he had and bought that field. MATT 13:44

Introduction

The lessons on Living the Parable will help you think through what you've learned about the parables in order to apply it to your daily life. Each lesson will include a transcript of the pastor's application video so you can review what he said on your own. It will also provide you with related verses from the Bible for further study and reflection.

Everyone is at a different place in his or her walk with the Lord. It is our belief that praying for guidance from the Holy Spirit, studying the Word of God, and then considering how it applies to our specific circumstances are some of the best ways to grow in grace as we live out the life of the Kingdom.

For this first Living the Parable chapter, the speaker's transcript will be followed by a brief discussion of the four questions that Dr. Daniel Doriani uses in his book *Putting the Truth to Work: The Theory and Practice of Biblical Application.* *Modern Parables* has used a number of the things he teaches in that book as the foundation for the Living the Parable sections. If you are interested in further study on the area of Biblical application, we would encourage you to read Dr. Doriani's book.

TRANSCRIPT OF APPLICATION VIDEO

Living out Hidden Treasure – Dr. Daniel Doriani

Dr. Daniel Doriani is Senior Pastor of Central Presbyterian Church in St. Louis, Missouri.

Introduction

When I saw this property on screen I thought to myself, "That's one ugly piece of land." And now that I'm standing here, I have to tell you this is urban blight at its worst. This is one ugly piece of property. And that set me thinking. It's very different to watch something on a screen compared to experiencing it in person. It's one thing to live, it's another thing simply to watch.

For example, it's very different to watch a picture of a waterfall as opposed to feeling the spray in your face and the roar in your ears. Seeing versus experiencing—they're different things.

Why Jesus Taught in Parables

That difference between experiencing something and simply watching it is one of the main reasons why Jesus taught in parables. He didn't want to teach things that would enter our minds and then be filed away as some fact that we knew. He wanted to tell us stories that would enter our imaginations, that would enter our bones. We feel ourselves getting into the story, not just to live the story, but to hear what He said, to understand His teachings about the Kingdom of God and to act on them.

At first blush, Jesus' parables are just interesting little stories—relatively simple at first reading. But then you notice something strange happens in the parable, something that teases your mind into thought. You wonder, "Why did Jesus put that in the story? What does it mean? What does it mean to me?"

After a while you begin to realize why Jesus taught in parables. He told these stories so they would force you to think—so they would be like a small pebble in your shoe. Even the last thought before you go to bed at night is one more reflection on that parable. Then you realize that was His purpose in the first place: to make you think, to make you enter, to make you live—really live—what's in the parable.

Explaining Parables

So what exactly are parables?

They're simply comparisons that Jesus used that teach important truths about the Kingdom of God. This particular parable teaches us four different things about the Kingdom of God. The first is that the Kingdom is priceless. The second is that the Kingdom reveals itself to us often unexpectedly. Third, when it does, we should take radical, decisive action to acquire the Kingdom. Finally, when we do acquire the Kingdom—or maybe we could say it acquires us—it transforms everything.

When it comes down to it, the parable of the Hidden Treasure is about a very simple question: once we realize the supreme value of the Kingdom, will we enter it? Will we live faithfully before the King?

The Four Questions

As we apply the parables to the Kingdom of God and life in the Kingdom, there are four aspects of application of our studies. I'd like to phrase them as "the four questions people ask." They are four questions people have asked throughout the ages—philosophers, ethicists—and they certainly also appear in the Bible. In fact, the Bible teaches us to ask these questions, and it gives us abundant answers to them.

The first question is "What is my duty?" What should I do? What does God require of me? What behavior is specified in the Law of God? What do the Ten Commandments require? What does Jesus require in His teachings? What does God require as a bare minimum for our actions? That's the first question: What's my duty? What should I do?

The second question is "What should I be?" or the question of character. The question of character—who should I be—touches on our ability to do what God requires us to do. In other words, we all know that we can't simply resolve to do whatever we wish. All of us have experienced those times when we want to do something, but we find that we can't. Or we do it for a little while, but then we peter out—we don't persevere. How can I actually have the capacity to persevere in the obedience that God wants of me? How can I achieve virtue? How can I be a loving and kind and gracious and generous person? That's the question of character.

The third question is the question of goals, or the question, "Where should I go?" The first and second questions are answered the same way for everybody. Everybody has the same duties, everyone should pursue the same godly character. But then, when it comes to our goals, they are unique for each one of us. God has given each one of us particular gifts, experiences, skills, teachers, even failures, that uniquely prepare us for what He wants us to do.

How do I figure out what my gifts, what my experiences, what my passions are, what's unique in the way God has made me? What will lead me into the projects and the kinds of things that I'll invest my life's energy in?

The fourth question is that of vision or discernment: "How can I learn to see the world God's way?" Now we know that the Lord gives His absolute truth in the Bible, but His truth is challenged in so many ways in our culture. There are other religions such as Islam or Buddhism. Beyond that there are agnostics and atheists and naturalists. And they're all putting forward their claims.

Even people who aren't philosophers are simply saying, "Hey, enjoy the good life. Live for pleasure. Live for achievement. Live for recognition." How can I understand yet disregard and screen out those false voices? How can I hear the truth and see the world God's way? How can I discern His voice among all the others?

Those are the four basic questions the Bible teaches us to ask in so many ways. We will consistently apply those four questions to the parables as pathways to application.

Purchasing the Kingdom

So what does the parable of the Hidden Treasure require in regard to our duty? It's very clear: the parable requires that we use decisive action to enter the Kingdom of God. Jesus said, "Seek first the kingdom and God's righteousness." This parable requires us to be willing to take the radical action of selling everything—giving up everything, paying any price—to enter the Kingdom of God.

The second question concerns our character: who should we be? This parable answers that we should be men and women who have the kind of character that is able to take decisive action to enter the Kingdom of God. We need to see an opportunity and take advantage of it quickly. Even further, we need to be willing to give up what is most precious to us in order to acquire the Kingdom.

Third, we have to think about our goals. The parable of the Hidden Treasure really makes one simple point: until we actually do enter the Kingdom of Heaven, the main goal we have in life is to enter the Kingdom. We have to be willing to do whatever it takes, make any sacrifice, endure the ridicule, even the scorn, of friends and relatives. We should be willing to pay any price to finish the race in order to win the prize.

Finally, let's talk about wisdom or discernment. Let's not do it through a series of statements, but rather through questions. The first question this parable teaches us to ask is, "What is of true worth? What is of supreme value?" And beyond that, once we as Christians accept the supreme value of the Kingdom, do we sometimes reacquire those things that we once sacrificed for the Kingdom? How, in short, can we forget what the Kingdom of God is worth?

If you're watching this story today, it's possible that you aren't sure that you're a member of the Kingdom of God. Now is the time to ask if you're not sure. Ask your teacher, ask your pastor, ask a friend. This study may be God Himself revealing His Kingdom to you at this hour. It could be time for you to act—to act decisively so that you can live in the Kingdom of God.

It's also possible that you're watching this video and you are a child of God—you are living in the Kingdom. But as you think about the cost that the man in this story paid, you realize you haven't done anything radical or risky like that for a long time. You've been assuming – you've even been presuming – on God. It may be time for you to recommit yourself so that you'll live truly in the Kingdom of God.

AN OVERVIEW OF LIVING THE PARABLES

Knowing and Doing

We who live in the West have perfected the art of knowing without doing. Many of us can discourse intelligently on the Bible and God's commands while ignoring them on a daily basis. Of course, we are not the first culture to do so. Some Pharisees in Jesus' day had also been infected with this kind of thinking. As Jesus pointed out: "The teachers of the law and the Pharisees sit in Moses' seat. So you must obey them and do everything they tell you. But do not do what they do, for they do not practice what they preach." (Matt 23:2-3)

This idea of practicing what we preach often makes us un-comfortable. The fact is, if we really did everything we said we believed it would make our lives look very different. There is a general level of comfort that we live in which would likely be disturbed if we did exactly what we say we believe about taking care of the poor, tithing, loving our neighbor and so forth.

Jesus knew that hypocrisy is endemic to all people. And one of His primary means of combating pervasive hypocrisy was the parable.

After all, the whole point of teaching in parables was to drive His followers to change their lives in light of the Kingdom of God. It does us no good to listen to the parable of the Good Samaritan, agree that it is important to love our neigh-bors as ourselves, and yet not love our neighbors more. To do so merely means that we don't understand the parable.

Now some people may say that we can't change our lives ourselves, that we are sinful, and that the Holy Spirit must do this for us. That is true. But as C.S. Lewis pointed out, we do have the dignity of causality (in other words, *we can do things*). And if we are regenerate (or saved) then the Holy Spirit is working in us. Jesus, Paul and the epistle writers all used im-perative verbs on a regular basis: *love* your enemies; *be* holy; *forgive* others. We not only *have* the ability to do these things, we are *expected* to do them as followers of Christ. If we do not do them, we are in sin.

We are talking here about living as Christians on a day-to-day basis. We are talking about the choices we make from the moment we wake up to the moment we go to sleep. We are talking about money, about prayer, about love, about trust, and about all the other things that come with being part of the Kingdom of God. All these things are the primary subjects of the parables. It was exactly because Jesus knew that these things would be the bread and butter of our lives that He told us parables about them. Our responsibility is to incorporate the parables into our daily lives.

Four Aspects of Living the Parables

In normal Christian parlance, we often talk about applying the Scripture to our lives. *Application* is putting something into operation, actually doing something. But it also suggests a conscious effort, something we have to think about and do.

The idea of *living*, however, is much more basic. Living is what we do whether we think about it or not. It's the basic level of our being. If we're not living, well... you get the picture.

Living is just the daily outworking of life. And Jesus tells us over and over again that true life is found only in Him: "For just as the Father raises the dead and gives them life, even so the Son gives life to whom he is pleased to give it." (John 5:21) What is this life, and how does it work into our daily living?

At its base, this life is *knowing God.* (John 17:3) But knowing God is not a static thing; rather it manifests itself in an ongoing, redemptive relationship with God as He changes us from being naturally sinful to naturally holy (a process also known as sanctification). Dr. Daniel Doriani has identified four aspects of living in God's Kingdom that are manifested in our living out the commands and principles found in the Bible.[1] He has expressed them as four questions:

1   What should I do? That is, what is my <u>duty</u>?
2   Who should I be? That is, how can I become the person or obtain the <u>character</u> that lets me do what is right?
3   To what causes should I devote my life energy? That is, what <u>goals</u> should I pursue?
4   How can I distinguish truth from error? That is, how can I gain <u>discernment</u>?[2]

We will briefly look at each of the questions here:

I. WHAT SHOULD I DO? THAT IS, WHAT IS MY <u>DUTY</u>?
The moral life begins with commands. As Jesus Himself said,
"If anyone loves me, he will obey my teaching" (John 14:23)
and "Blessed rather are those who hear the word of God and
obey it." (Luke 11:28) Jesus expects us to obey His commands.
It's our duty to love others, to give to the poor, to love God.
In a Biblical sense, duty is what is expected of us. Duty is the
ground floor where we all have to start.

There is a lot of controversy today about the idea of
duty. Some Christians warn against being too consumed
with duty; others see it as the key to a happy life. The fact is,
were there no sin in the world, we would all naturally do our
duties (loving God and loving our neighbor) and there would
be no debate. However, our sinfulness can take the principle
of duty and make it a means of personal salvation or condemnation (legalism) or we can rebel against it and make it a hated
concept (antinomianism).

But let's look at an example of duty put in the proper Biblical perspective. It is the duty of a husband and wife to love one
another. Assuming they have a healthy relationship, it is an easy
thing to love one another. Their duty can be very enjoyable and
not seem to be a "duty" at all (evidence that the word itself has
taken on bad connotations). Of course, if a husband and wife
are in a fight and have sinned against each other, the duty of loving one another can be onerous and even impossible. The Holy
Spirit is required in both instances: in the first instance, the
Spirit was actively involved in the pleasant doing of their duty;
in the second, one or both were sinning against the Spirit and
needed conviction and change. The point here is not that the
duty is altered, but that *sin affects the exercise of duty.*

Doriani explains it well: "By schooling people in their
duty we establish a necessary minimum standard for conduct."[3]
And the concerns about falling into legalism? "The best way to
combat legalism is to join duty and character. Character bal-
ances duty by stifling the notion that Christian living consists in

adherence to a set of rules."[4] And it helps us realize that we live the Christian life fundamentally in gratitude to God for saving us in a way we could never have done ourselves.

2. WHO SHOULD I BE? THAT IS, HOW CAN I BECOME THE PERSON OR OBTAIN THE CHARACTER THAT LETS ME DO WHAT IS RIGHT?

If duty is about what we *should* be doing, then character is about who we should *be*. It concerns the state of our hearts, our internal nature. Jesus explained it as: "The good man brings good things out of the good stored up in his heart, and the evil man brings evil things out of the evil stored up in his heart." (Luke 6:45) Our character directly influences our actions; in fact, it is the source of our actions.

This does not mean that our character is static. Rather, due to the sin in our hearts, our character is flawed at its source. Were it not, we would naturally do the duties and obey the laws required of us. The Holy Spirit, however, is continuously sanctifying our character in order for us to do what God wants us to do. As Paul tells us, "But if Christ is in you, your body is dead because of sin, yet your spirit is alive because of righteousness. And if the Spirit of him who raised Jesus from the dead is living in you, he who raised Christ from the dead will also give life to your mortal bodies through his Spirit, who lives in you." (Rom 8:10-11)

In other words, our character is constantly being pulled between our sinful nature and our new nature in Christ. Not being robots, we do have the ability to choose between these two options. Our choices not only spring from our character, but progressively influence our character on a long-term basis.

Ultimately, the Holy Spirit is transforming our characters to reflect the character of Christ. As Paul tells us in Corinthians, "And we, who with unveiled faces all reflect the Lord's glory, are being transformed into his likeness with ever-increasing glory, which comes from the Lord, who is the Spirit." (2 Cor 3:18)

3. TO WHAT CAUSES SHOULD I DEVOTE MY LIFE ENERGY? THAT IS, WHAT <u>GOALS</u> SHOULD I PURSUE? The two preceding aspects of living out the parables, duty and character, were personal in nature. They related primarily to us as individuals. These two aspects are the twin foundations of living in the Kingdom of God, but they must naturally grow outward into the *goals* God has for our lives.

History shows us that God is redeeming this sinful world through the work of His servants. One need only glance at the ways Christianity has impacted the world for good to see how He is doing this: civil laws, hospitals, orphanages, art, business practices, and so forth. God is redeeming the world not only through changing the inner lives of people, but by using those people to alter the institutions and cultures of the world through the choices they make for their lives.

A classic example of this is William Wilberforce, the member of British parliament who set as his life goal the abolishment of slavery in the British Empire. He used the skills that God had given him and the position that God had put him in to push forward the Kingdom of God in a specific and important way.

Let us not forget that we are living in the midst of an enormous war. There are two kingdoms in conflict, and, as Christians, we are the soldiers fighting Christ's battles with Him. This is the meaning of David's prophecy concerning Jesus: "The LORD will extend your mighty scepter from Zion; you will rule in the midst of your enemies. Your troops will be willing on your day of battle." (Psa 110:2-3) Paul confirms this when he tells Timothy, "Endure hardship with us like a good soldier of Christ Jesus." (2 Tim 2:3)

In light of this, the choices that we make in terms of our daily work, our friendships, our hobbies, our places of worship, our missions activities, our evangelism, our service to others, our recreation – all these choices relate to the goals we have set for ourselves. The daily choices we make are not inconsequential. A building is built one brick at a time.

But, as Klaas Schilder pointed out, there are only two pos-sible uses of those bricks.[5] For example, one brick is used to build an abortion clinic while another brick is used to build a church. In our daily decisions, we are following goals that support the growth of either the Kingdom of God or the kingdom of Satan. There is no middle ground.

The parables force us to examine our goals, and then to set them in light of the Kingdom of God. "Pursuing the right goals, we improve our corner of the world and feel God's pleasure at our actions."[6]

4. HOW CAN WE DISTINGUISH TRUTH FROM ERROR? THAT IS, HOW CAN WE GAIN DISCERNMENT? Solomon admonishes us in Proverbs to "preserve sound judgment and discernment, do not let them out of your sight; they will be life for you, an ornament to grace your neck." (Prov 3:21-22) In this sense, discernment is directly related to Biblical wisdom. It is "the insight...to see things as they are from God's perspective."[7]

In our daily lives there are countless things that com-pete for our attention. We are constantly making decisions between competing duties, competing character issues, and competing goals. As often as not, the choice isn't between good and bad, but between good and better. It is the attri-bute of discernment that helps us to *see through* the issues to what God would have us do at that particular moment.

The Bible is clear that it is the Spirit who gives us dis-cernment. Paul tells the Ephesians that "I keep asking that the God of our Lord Jesus Christ...may give you the Spirit of wisdom." (Eph 1:17) Biblical discernment helps us to look at our culture and see what is edifying and what is not. It helps us look at our work and see what is godly and what is not. It helps us look at our relationships and see what is Biblical and what is not.

In our day and age discernment for daily living is a

necessity. The parables teach us to think God's thoughts in relation to the world and to see things with His *worldview*. Such a worldview often means that we will be going against the grain not only with those outside of God's Kingdom, but even with those lacking discernment *within* His Kingdom. It is to this end that Paul encourages us "that your love may abound more and more in knowledge and depth of insight, so that you may be able to *discern* what is best and may be pure and blameless until the day of Christ." (Phil 1:9-11)

ADDITIONAL VERSES FOR STUDY AND REFLECTION

MATTHEW 13:44-46

"The kingdom of heaven is like treasure hidden in a field. When a man found it, he hid it again, and then in his joy went and sold all he had and bought that field.

"Again, the kingdom of heaven is like a merchant looking for fine pearls. When he found one of great value, he went away and sold everything he had and bought it."

*   *   *

LUKE 18:18-30

A certain ruler asked [Jesus], "Good teacher, what must I do to inherit eternal life?"

"Why do you call me good?" Jesus answered. "No one is good—except God alone. You know the commandments: 'Do not commit adultery, do not murder, do not steal, do not give false testimony, honor your father and mother.'"

"All these I have kept since I was a boy," he said.

When Jesus heard this, he said to him, "You still lack one thing. Sell everything you have and give to the poor, and you will have treasure in heaven. Then come, follow me."

When he heard this, he became very sad, because he was a man of great wealth. Jesus looked at him and said, "How hard it is for the rich to enter the kingdom of God! Indeed, it is easier for a camel to go through the eye of a needle than for a rich man to enter the kingdom of God."

Those who heard this asked, "Who then can be saved?"

Jesus replied, "What is impossible with men is possible with God."

Peter said to him, "We have left all we had to follow you!"

"I tell you the truth," Jesus said to them, "no one who has left home or wife or brothers or parents or children for the sake of the kingdom of God will fail to receive many times as much in this age and, in the age to come, eternal life."

*   *   *

PROVERBS 8:12-21

"I, wisdom, dwell together with prudence; I possess knowledge and discretion. To fear the LORD is to hate evil; I hate pride and arrogance, evil behavior and perverse speech. Counsel and sound judgment are mine; I have understanding and power. By me kings reign and rulers make laws that are just; by me princes govern, and all nobles who rule on earth. I love those who love me, and those who seek me find me. With me are riches and honor, enduring wealth and prosperity. My fruit is better than fine gold; what I yield surpasses choice silver. I walk in the way of righteousness, along the paths of justice, bestowing wealth on those who love me and making their treasuries full."

Endnotes

1 Daniel M. Doriani, *Putting the Truth to Work* (P&R Publishing, 2001) 97.

2 Doriani, 98.

3 Doriani, 104.

4 Doriani, 105.

5 Klaas Schilder, *Christ and Culture* (G. van Rongen and W. Helder, 1977) 72.

6 Doriani, 110.

7 Doriani, 114.

Luke 10:25-37

Samaritan

UNDERSTANDING THE PARABLE

*On one occasion an expert in the law stood up to test Jesus. "Teacher,"
he asked, "what must I do to inherit eternal life?"*

"What is written in the Law?" he replied. "How do you read it?"

*He answered: " 'Love the Lord your God with all your heart and with
all your soul and with all your strength and with all your mind'; and,
'Love your neighbor as yourself.' "*

*"You have answered correctly," Jesus replied. "Do this and you
will live."*

*But he wanted to justify himself, so he asked Jesus, "And who is
my neighbor?"*

*In reply Jesus said: "A man was going down from Jerusalem to
Jericho, when he fell into the hands of robbers. They stripped him of
his clothes, beat him and went away, leaving him half dead. A priest
happened to be going down the same road, and when he saw the man,
he passed by on the other side. So too, a Levite, when he came to the
place and saw him, passed by on the other side. But a Samaritan, as
he traveled, came where the man was; and when he saw him, he took
pity on him. He went to him and bandaged his wounds, pouring on
oil and wine. Then he put the man on his own donkey, took him to
an inn and took care of him. The next day he took out two silver coins*

and gave them to the innkeeper. 'Look after him,' he said, 'and when
I return, I will reimburse you for any extra expense you may have.'

"Which of these three do you think was a neighbor to the man who
fell into the hands of robbers?"

The expert in the law replied, "The one who had mercy on him."

Jesus told him, "Go and do likewise."   LUKE 10:25-37

Introduction

The parable of the Good Samaritan is one of the most well-
known parables in the Bible. Its influence is so wide that in
the United States and Canada statutes exist known as Good
Samaritan laws. These laws are intended to make it easier for
passersby to stop and help someone injured without worrying about legal repercussions. The word "Samaritan" itself is
considered a compliment: "You were such a Samaritan for
stopping and helping that lady change her tire."

But it hasn't always been that way.

As we approach the parable of the Good Samaritan, we
need to understand what the first-century audience listening
to Jesus would have immediately thought about the various
characters involved in the story. His listeners would have had
very different opinions than we do today about this parable.
Just as you may have felt a little uneasy at the end of the film,
so too would many of Jesus' listeners at the end of His story.

An Expert's Question

Luke provides us with a description of one particular listener: the expert in the law who asked Jesus the two questions
that eventually led to the parable. Although most people just
look at the parable itself, it is important to recognize the real-
world situation that bookends the story. As we just read, the
expert in the law stood up to ask Jesus a question. This expert
was not like our law experts of today. Also known as a "scribe"
or "doctor of the law," the first-century Jewish lawyers were a
class of professional jurists, almost more like roving judges.

Their job was to interpret the many laws passed down to them from their forefathers. The scribes of Jesus' day had the job of trying to make sense of all the various interpretations of the Mosaic law that had grown up over the centuries. They often discussed these thorny issues in groups, sometimes quite legitimately grappling with what was the truth.

When Jesus entered this legal world, His quite radical interpretation of the law caused a stir among many of these same lawyers. He made strong and powerful statements about interpreting the law — and not always to everyone's liking. It was in this context that one of these experts stood up to ask Him the controversial question "How does one inherit eternal life?" In a sense, this would be similar to the question that someone might ask today, "How is one saved?" The assumption that the expert was making, as is also common today, is that we can *do* something to inherit eternal life. He wanted to know: what does one need to do?[1]

But instead of answering his question, Jesus asked a question in reply. This method of returning a question with a question was quite common in that day. Jesus asked him how he interpreted the law. The expert replied with the classic statement summarizing the law. It is a combination of two verses from the Old Testament — Deuteronomy 6:5 (love God) and Leviticus 19:18 (love your neighbor) — which Jesus Himself used in another instance.

Upon hearing the expert say this, Jesus immediately commended the man for having spoken the truth. But saying the right thing and doing the right thing are not the same thing. No doubt that is why Jesus followed His congratulatory remark with the command: "Do this, and you will live." Following the greatest commandment brings life *now*, as well as in the future. Of course, Jesus well knew that even though all must follow this law, our sinful nature makes it impossible for us to follow it completely. How can you love God with all your heart all the time? And your neighbor as yourself? Impossible! The impossibility, however, does not change the fact that we are required to follow the whole law.[2]

Yet, instead of questioning Jesus in that direction, the expert brought up what was most likely an ongoing discussion between the scribes concerning the interpretation of this word "neighbor."[3] "Who is my neighbor?" That is, who does the term neighbor really apply to? Everyone agreed that it included all natural Jews, but what about gentiles who had converted to Judaism? Did they fall under this definition? And, of course, there were the unbelieving gentiles. But almost everyone at the time agreed that this law didn't include anyone outside the genealogical nation of Israel. Furthermore, many interpreted the law to mean that those who were enemies of the Jews should not be helped at all even if they were in need. Unbelievers couldn't be neighbors under this definition.

In first-century Israel, there were many people who were not Jews by blood or beliefs: Romans, Greeks, Samaritans, Egyptians, Persians, etc. Israel was the cross-roads of trade between Africa and the Middle East, so many races and religions could be found in this little country of the Jews.

And so it was into this racially and religiously divided situation that Jesus answered the expert's second question with His parable. It soon became apparent that the expert's view of loving one's neighbor was woefully inadequate in comparison to the Biblical standard.

The Hurt Man

A man was going down from Jerusalem to Jericho, when he fell into the hands of robbers. They stripped him of his clothes, beat him and went away, leaving him half dead. LUKE 10:30

Jerusalem was the capital of Judea and was located in the mountain chain running north-south through the country.

To the east the land dipped down into the Jordan river valley and met the Jordan river. Jericho lay near this river and was the first city Joshua destroyed with the Israelites over 1500 years before when they first entered the land. The particular road is a real road about 17 miles long; it descends all the way from Jerusalem to Jericho.[4] It was well known that the road was infested with robbers and thieves. When the Romans first invaded Israel and conquered it, Pompey the Great sent a series of legions to kill all the thieves and clean up the roads. Nevertheless, due to the terrain as well as the constant travel on it, it was always a good place to find easy victims.

In Jesus' parable, the man was beaten, robbed, and left to die, as well as stripped of his clothes. Although the people listening would not have been surprised at this bitter detail (clothes were generally considered to be more valuable than they are today), some indirect assumptions were based on it. First, Jesus' listeners would have assumed the man was a Jew since both they and Jesus were. Jesus would likely have stated the race of the man if he had been anything else. Furthermore, once someone was stripped of his clothes while unconscious, he became virtually unidentifiable since, just like today, clothing and accent were two primary ways of identifying people.[5] It wouldn't be too out of the ordinary to hear about someone being beaten and left on the side of Jericho road. It would be like hearing about someone getting mugged in the inner city today: it's not really uncommon news.

This is where the film begins. After a mugging in a downtown area, the victim is in a similar situation — helpless, unknown and unidentifiable. The one common factor in both stories is that anyone passing by can see that a person is hurt. The question, of course, is will someone stop and help?

In Jesus' parable, the word translated "half-dead" meant that the man wasn't dead yet, but very close.[6] In other words, he's in critical condition. It is likely that the people who come upon him arrive not long after he has been hurt.

The First Passerby: The Priest

*A priest happened to be going down the same road, and when he saw
the man, he passed by on the other side.* LUKE 10:31

The first to arrive is a priest. The priests were the top level of
the religious class in Jewish society. They served at the temple
on an annual basis, offering sacrifices to God on behalf of
the people. Priests were known to be some of the wealthiest
citizens in Jewish society, and so the listeners would have assumed this priest would have been riding a donkey or horse.
A priest would not have been walking seventeen miles through
the desert on foot.[7]

In this instance, the priest sees the man and immediately
steers to the other side of the road. He doesn't even bother
to examine him. Some of Jesus' listeners would have nodded
in cynical recognition: another rich man passing by someone
in distress. But as they considered this, they would have been
aware of something a modern-day reader would probably miss.
In that day, everyone would have known that a priest could
become unclean by touching a dead body, and hence unfit
for temple service. In fact, in order to return to a clean state,
he would have had to take the humiliating role of standing
in a certain gate of the city with the other unclean (and socially
unacceptable) for a set period of time. Furthermore, it would
actually cost him money to make the specific sacrifices necessary
to return to ceremonial purity.[8] In his mind, he could use
a strict interpretation of the law to justify his inaction on
account of his job, his status, and his finances. Some of Jesus'
listeners would no doubt have understood this, and perhaps
felt sympathy for the priest's situation.

But not much. Jesus' parable suggests the priest didn't
even take the time to see how hurt the man really was. Even
worse, as a minister at the temple, his job was to intercede
for the people as their spiritual representative before God. In

other words, he of all people should be interested in a person's welfare. But instead he sticks to his own business and lets the man lie there, dying and hopeless. In his own mind, he could justify ignoring the man as his neighbor by a twisted interpretation of the law that required him to remain physically uncontaminated.

In the film, a deacon in the church – who is also a medical doctor – first encounters the old man lying against the wall. Again, this is not uncommon in our own day: many of us have passed drunks in the city. Although his son Peter initially draws his attention to the man, it is the father's decision to leave him. As a deacon, an important part of his role in the church is to take care of the sick and needy; as a doctor, his role in society is to take care of the hurt and dying. He justifies his inaction by his need to get to work as well as by the man's presumed condition: he's old, he's lying against a wall in the morning with blood on his face – he's probably drunk. It would be a little humiliating to put the old man in the car and drive him to the emergency room; it would smell bad and he would probably get blood on his seats. In the deacon's mind, he could justify ignoring the man as his neighbor by a twisted set of societal rules some tacitly follow: I've got important things to do, it would take a lot of time to deal with him, and he's really in that condition as a result of his own actions. He follows an interpretation of the law that encourages him to remain socially uncontaminated.

The Second Passerby: The Levite

So too, a Levite, when he came to the place and saw him, passed by on the other side. LUKE 10:32

In Jesus' parable, a Levite arrives next on the scene. The Levites were also a religious class that served at the temple, but were lower in status and wealth. In this case, the Levite is following the priest in the same direction, perhaps because he, too, is returning from his regular temple service.

It is here that we must mention a topographical note about the road on which everyone is traveling. We who drive regularly at high speeds are not used to the slower pace of ancient travel. This particular road was long and straight. Those who have traveled it say that it is easy to see for miles along the road; furthermore, because it was known to be dangerous, people kept a keen eye as to who was ahead of them on the road. In light of the man's extreme injuries, the listeners would likely have assumed that the Levite knew the Priest was on the road, and that the Levite had seen him pass the man. Since the Priest held a higher rank than the Levite, he would naturally have been seen as an authority figure. This would have had no small amount of influence on the Levite's actions.[9]

Nevertheless, the text says that the Levite "came to the place and saw him." Some scholars believe that the Levite got much closer to the man than the Priest did due to the language in the original text.[10] He would have inspected his wounds and seen he was truly hurt. But he would have been faced with a dilemma: should he help the man when the priest did not? To make things more difficult, since he was of a lower class, he could have been walking. He knew he certainly couldn't move the man. Even more, he too could be made unclean by touching a dead body (although it's likely he knew the man wasn't dead since he came so close). Although the cost for being made unclean was less than that of a priest, it was still an annoyance. How much easier it would be just to leave him!

In the film, this is the situation with James, the youth leader. Of a lower status than the deacon, he knows for certain that this authority figure saw the man and could have helped him. The deacon, after all, is a doctor; had the man needed help, he would have stopped and helped. Yet when James examines the man with his own eyes, it seems that he is truly hurt.

But James has immediate pressures on him: three boys who are his responsibility. It would be so much easier just to leave the man and do what he has planned on doing. Were he actually to stop and help, it would mean upsetting his plans, possibly canceling them. And he has an obligation to watch over these boys. The fact is, he just doesn't have time to help out an old drunk.

So he, too, leaves the man by the side of the road.

The Third Passerby: The Samaritan

But a Samaritan, as he traveled, came where the man was; and when
he saw him, he took pity on him. LUKE 10:33

In Jesus' parable, the last person to arrive is a Samaritan. For us reading this today, we are so familiar with the story that we are expecting this non-Jewish foreigner to be the hero. But that's not what Jesus' first-century audience would have thought. They would have been shocked and a touch horrified that the hero of the story was a—dare they even say it—Samaritan! After all, the Samaritans were a hated group of half-breeds who had fought against the Jews ever since they had returned from the Babylonian captivity 500 years before. To call someone a "Samaritan" was an insult. The Samaritans were a nasty race as far as the Jews were concerned.

And perhaps they had good cause for thinking so. The Samaritans were descended from a group of non-Jews who had been forcibly settled in the land after the Jewish inhabitants were banished and removed by the Assyrian empire in 722BC. The races that settled in the area intermarried with the remaining Jews. They followed a mixed religion that didn't recognize Jerusalem as being God's holy city, nor the Jews as God's people. When the Jews returned from captivity the Samaritans tried to keep them from rebuilding the temple. In Jesus' own time, they often denied Him and His disciples passage through their cities (causing James and John to ask Jesus to call down fire from heaven to destroy them). And not long before Jesus started His ministry, the Samaritans had scattered human bones in the Temple during a Passover, a highly offensive act comparable to burning a cross in front of a church. This was not a friendly rivalry.

Jesus is thus playing on one of His audience's deepest hatreds. It would be one thing to have a Jew help out a Samaritan, but a Samaritan help out a Jew? It was an appalling thought.[11]

And so in our film it is not an American Christian who stops and helps out the hurt man, but an Arab. Like the Samaritan in the story, we do not know exactly what he believes; but we do know that the people listening would have assumed the Samaritan followed a heretical religion, just as we assume that our Arab friend is a Muslim whose religion is equally heretical. Whereas the ones who should have stopped did not, the one who should not have stopped, did. What are we to make of this? What was Jesus' audience to make of this?

It was highly troubling to say the least. It exposed not only their mistaken notion of whom their neighbor was, but also their prejudice. It should have been the Priest and Levite who helped, not the Samaritan. It should have been the Deacon and Youth Leader who helped, not the Arab taxi driver.

The fact that the Samaritan in the film is an Arab immigrant is not meant to imply that Arab-Americans are "the enemy" in the way that Samaritans in Jesus' day were the enemies of the Jews. Rather, the Arab character is used because the suspicions that many American Christians harbor toward Arabs in the post-9/11 era most closely approximates the suspicions that Jews harbored toward Samaritans. If we find it somewhat disturbing that it is the Arab taxi driver who has pity when the two others do not, then we are feeling the same tension that Jesus' original listeners felt.

But what is this "pity" that the Samaritan shows? In the original language it is the word "compassion," and it is a very strong word that means to feel deeply. The Samaritan was deeply moved in his heart with compassion for the hurt man, and acted to help him. The Samaritan would likely have known that the Priest and Levite passed the man, but that doesn't stop him. Instead, he is most concerned about helping the man.

He, too, risks ceremonial contamination like the Priest and the Levite (and if a merchant, it would extend to his products and animals) if the man is dead.[12] But this does not matter. He comes to the man, moved solely by love.

> *He went to him and bandaged his wounds, pouring on oil and wine.*
> *Then he put the man on his own donkey, took him to an inn and*
> *took care of him. The next day he took out two silver coins and*
> *gave them to the innkeeper. 'Look after him,' he said, 'and when I*
> *return, I will reimburse you for any extra expense you may have.'*
> LUKE 10: 34-36

The Samaritan's first action is to bandage up the man. If we look at the verse, it is interesting to note the order of what he does: it says he bandages his wounds, then pours on oil and wine. First, it was common in those days to use oil to soften a blood-scabbed wound, to use wine to disinfect it, then finally to bandage it. Yet oil and wine are also the same things that the Priest and Levite would have used at the temple in their sacrificial rituals. Daily drink offerings were made to God in the Temple using oil and wine.[13] There is thus an ironic symbolism here that harkens back to God's message to Hosea saying, "For I desire mercy, not sacrifice, and acknowledgement of God rather than burnt offerings." (Hosea 6:6) The superficial use of things is never pleasing to God; rather, He wants His followers to love others and love Him. This is the true nature of sacrifice, as Paul himself tells us in Romans 12:1. The picture here is that God will use the instruments of worship how He chooses in the hands of the one He chooses, even a rejected outsider.[14]

We see in our own film that the taxi driver brings water to wash off the man's wounds, water being a classic symbol of cleansing inside the church. Although both the Deacon and Youth Minister had likely been washed in the water of baptism, this becomes a reminder that our baptism into Christ should drive us to help others.

The Inn

The Samaritan puts the man on his own donkey, just as the taxi driver puts him in his own vehicle (likely getting blood on the seat) and takes him to an inn. In Jesus' day there were no hospitals like we have today, so an inn was as good a place as any to let the man rest and recover (*hospital, hospitality, hostel,* and *hotel,* after all, come from the same root). The Samaritan took his own money to take care of the man; in the same way, our taxi driver passed up a fare.

We come now to the inn itself. Imagine the scene: a person who is generally treated with suspicion brings in someone hurt and helpless. Did he do it? Was he a part of this? Some commentators have pointed out that for a Samaritan to bring a Jew into a Jewish city and Jewish inn would have taken courage, and would likely have been met with suspicion and scorn. In the same way our taxi driver was looked at with suspicion.[15]

Nevertheless, the Samaritan says that he will be back to get him when he returns. And we can only assume that the man he saved would have been very happy to see him after all that he had done for him. Jesus' story ends just before we get to that point, but our film goes a little further, showing the hurt man picked up and taken by the taxi driver back to the bus station to finish his journey.

This enables us to see Peter's reaction. And what about it? His reaction was not unlike those originally listening: surprise at who had helped the man (especially in light of who did not), and wonderment at what it meant. It was to this point exactly that Jesus wanted to take His listeners, and especially the expert in the law who had first framed the question to Him.

Conclusion

> *"Which of these three do you think was a neighbor to the man who fell into the hands of robbers?" The expert in the law replied, "The one who had mercy on him." Jesus told him, "Go and do likewise."*
> LUKE 10:37

After finishing His parable, Jesus turned to the expert and asked him to identify the one who was a neighbor. The expert, perhaps even considering the truth of Hosea 6:6, answered that it is the one who had mercy on him. Jesus told him to go and have mercy on those in need in the same manner.

Mercy. What an extraordinary thing it is. As we know from Hosea, God desires His followers to be merciful far more than to sacrifice to Him; in fact, being merciful is the sacrifice God demands.

But how does this relate to the lawyer's first question: What can I do to inherit eternal life? And is it really possible for us to truly be merciful as Jesus demands?

PARALLELS

ORIGINAL PARABLE	PARABLE FILM
Dangerous road to Jericho.	Inner city is a dangerous place.
Hurt man stripped of clothes and unidentifiable.	Hurt man assumed to be drunk and unidentifiable.
Priest: elite class, responsible for taking care of people spiritually.	Deacon/Doctor: elite class, responsible for taking care of the poor and hurt.
Religious uncleanness.	Social uncleanness.

Likely riding a horse or donkey.	Riding in a car.
Steering to the other side.	Not getting close enough to see.
Levite: middle class, with some spiritual responsibility.	Youth Leader: middle class, with some spiritual responsibility.
Likely on foot.	On foot.
Likely knew the priest was ahead of him and had already passed the man.	Knew the deacon had come first and had already passed the man.
Goes closer to examine the man.	Goes closer to examine the man.
Faces issues of uncleanness as well as difficulty of how to move him.	Faces social issues as well as not having a way to move him.
Likely influenced by priest's actions.	Likely influenced by deacon's actions.
Samaritans were a different race with recognizable characteristics.	Those of Arabic descent are of a different race, often recognizable.
Samaritans were hated by Jews and held in deep distrust.	Arabs sometimes disliked by Americans and distrusted.
Samaritanism was a religion based on Judaism, but heretical.	Islam is a religion based on Judaism and Christianity, but heretical.
The Samaritan used oil and wine to clean the man, symbolic of Jewish temple ritual.	The Arab used water to clean the man, symbolic of Christian baptismal ritual.
The Samaritan put him on his horse.	The Arab put him in his car.
The Samaritan stayed to take care of him.	The Arab stayed to ensure he was okay.

Those in the inn would have been suspicious of the Samaritan.	Those in the ER were suspicious of the Arab.
The Samaritan acted out of compassion.	The Arab acted out of compassion.

Endnotes

1   Kenneth Bailey, *Through Peasant Eyes* (Eerdman's, 1984) 36.

2   Bailey, 31.

3   Bailey, 40.

5   Bailey, 41.

5   Bailey, 42.

6   Ibid.

7   Bailey, 43.

8   Bailey, 45.

9   Bailey, 46.

10 Bailey, 46-47.

11 Bailey, 47.

12 Bailey, 48.

13 Bailey, 50.

14 Ibid.

15 Bailey, 51.

Luke 10:25-37

Samaritan

LIVING THE PARABLE

*On one occasion an expert in the law stood up to test Jesus. "Teacher,"
he asked, "what must I do to inherit eternal life?"*

"What is written in the Law?" he replied. "How do you read it?"

*He answered: " 'Love the Lord your God with all your heart and
with all your soul and with all your strength and with all your mind';
and, 'Love your neighbor as yourself.'"*

*"You have answered correctly," Jesus replied. "Do this and you
will live."*

*But he wanted to justify himself, so he asked Jesus, "And who is my
neighbor?"*

*In reply Jesus said: "A man was going down from Jerusalem to
Jericho, when he fell into the hands of robbers. They stripped him of
his clothes, beat him and went away, leaving him half dead. A priest
happened to be going down the same road, and when he saw the man,
he passed by on the other side. So too, a Levite, when he came to the
place and saw him, passed by on the other side. But a Samaritan, as
he traveled, came where the man was; and when he saw him, he took
pity on him. He went to him and bandaged his wounds, pouring on
oil and wine. Then he put the man on his own donkey, took him to
an inn and took care of him. The next day he took out two silver coins*

*and gave them to the innkeeper. 'Look after him,' he said, 'and when
I return, I will reimburse you for any extra expense you may have.'*

*"Which of these three do you think was a neighbor to the man who
fell into the hands of robbers?"*

The expert in the law replied, "The one who had mercy on him."

Jesus told him, "Go and do likewise." LUKE 10:25-37

TRANSCRIPT OF APPLICATION VIDEO

Living out Samaritan — Rev. Jeff Schulte

Rev. Jeff Schulte is a pastor at ChangePoint church in Anchorage, Alaska.

Introduction

When I hear the parable of the Good Samaritan, I feel a range
of emotions. I feel glad. I feel sad. I even feel angry. I put
myself in the shoes of the characters in the story and I wonder
what I would have felt—I wonder what I would have done. Or
more importantly, I wonder what I would do now.

Answering these questions, I believe, is the key to unlocking what Jesus Christ wanted us to see in this parable of the
Good Samaritan. In it a power is revealed that will unlock
in us a God-prompted love, compassion and mercy to those
people that God brings upon our path.

The Reality of Sin

The first reality we have to recognize is that sin is as real as
these bricks. It's not an abstract idea. And the consequences
of sin, or the effects of sin, are just as real. All we have to do
to know this is true is for us to look around. To look around—
but better yet, I know for myself, to look inside.

And when I look inside I know that sin has corrupted me—
it's corrupted all of us. Sure we'll admit we're sinners, but do
we recognize just how desperate our situation is? That were

it not for the grace of God, we would find ourselves—if not physically, at least metaphorically—in an alley like this man in the story, left for dead, desperately in need of help.

The Reality of Duty

We're too familiar with this parable, which is why it doesn't surprise us when those first two men don't stop to help. While it doesn't surprise us, it does still bother us. We put ourselves in the shoes of this doctor. And like him we can come up with a hundred reasons why we wouldn't stop to help. Rationalizing, justifying, and excusing ourselves out of doing our duty.

Duty. We don't like how this sounds or how this feels, yet we do judge these two men for not stopping to help. One is both a doctor and a deacon, so both by his calling as well as by his profession we know that he has committed to helping others. The other is a religious man, so he too would be committed to putting the needs of others above himself.

Yet isn't that what makes their inaction so intolerable? This is why when these first two travelers fail so miserably, we intuitively feel their guilt. We expect them—we want them—to be responsible for this man on the side of the road.

Let's put our two realities together. First, we know that sin is real and that it affects all of us. Second, we know it's our duty to love others. So do you see the problem? We know what it is that God expects of us, yet because of our sin, we become masters at not doing it. In fact, we can be so good at this, we can come up with reasons why it's the most loving thing to do nothing.

We know it's our duty to help, and we feel guilt. But do we feel love? And if we don't feel love, then it's because we're missing something.

The Law of Love

Remember the law of love. It says, "love your neighbor as you love yourself." This brings us to our third reality—he who has experienced the love of God will express the love of God. And he who has not experienced that love will not express it.

Let me say that again because that's what this is all about. The person who has experienced the love of God will be empowered to express that love. And the person who has not experienced the love of God will not be able to express it. That's why the first two men in this parable have such a difficult time carrying out their duty. They were so self-reliant, and so self-righteous, that they saw their need as just a little. Therefore they experienced the love of God just a little—and therefore had no capacity to give any of that love to anybody else.

There are two people in the New Testament that we see Jesus having the most difficult time with – the religious man and the wealthy man. Two groups of people that had a hard time seeing their need. Therefore two groups of people that could not experience the fullness of His love for them. And therefore two groups of people that had no ability to love anyone else.

Where does compassion come from? How is this kind of love grown in our hearts? We said that sin is real, and its effect upon us is just as real. We also know that it is our duty to love others, but that we will only love others to the extent that we have seen our own need and experienced love ourselves. We love because God first loved us.

The Love of Christ Flowing Through Us

The parable of the Good Samaritan is really a story about you, me, and Jesus. And it's not until we see ourselves as that battered and broken man on the side of the road that our hearts will be filled with compassion toward other wounded travelers who, like us, are in need of the love of Christ, expressed through the hands of Christ.

It's only when our hearts are flooded with the love of Christ, rushing in to fill the vacuum created by our need, that our hearts are warmed by His Holy Spirit, empowering us to move toward others, fulfilling the law of love. And that doesn't feel like duty. It feels like love because that's what it is. It is the love of Christ being poured out upon me and then through me, like a conduit, toward others in their place of greatest need.

Now I want to warn you, but then I'm going to encourage you. God isn't asking us to muster up some kind of self-will or inner fortitude that would cause us to love others—it just doesn't work that way. At least, not for very long. God isn't asking us to be God. He's asking us to come to Him with our need. And when He meets us in our place of need, we will find Him supernaturally working through us to meet others in their place of need.

To the extent that we find ourselves experiencing Him and our need of Him—to that extent we will find ourselves empowered to give that same love to others—to love others the way we love ourselves. And it's going to be in those moments—again, experiencing His love for us, and then expressing that same love for others—that we will be living, in the way Jesus described it, in the Kingdom of God.

ADDITIONAL VERSES
FOR STUDY AND REFLECTION

Hosea 6:1-6

"Come, let us return to the LORD.

He has torn us to pieces but he will heal us; he has injured us but he will bind up our wounds.

After two days he will revive us; on the third day he will restore us, that we may live in his presence.

Let us acknowledge the LORD; let us press on to acknowledge him.

As surely as the sun rises, he will appear; he will come to us like the winter rains, like the spring rains that water the earth."

"What can I do with you, Ephraim? What can I do with you, Judah?

Your love is like the morning mist, like the early dew that disappears.

Therefore I cut you in pieces with my prophets, I killed you with the words of my mouth; my judgments flashed like lightning upon you.

For I desire mercy, not sacrifice, and acknowledgment of God rather than burnt offerings."

*   *   *

MATTHEW 5:43-48

"You have heard that it was said, 'Love your neighbor and hate your enemy.' But I tell you: Love your enemies and pray for those who persecute you, that you may be sons of your Father in heaven. He causes his sun to rise on the evil and the good, and sends rain on the righteous and the unrighteous. If you love those who love you, what reward will you get? Are not even the tax collectors doing that? And if you greet only your brothers, what are you doing more than others? Do not even pagans do that? Be perfect, therefore, as your heavenly Father is perfect."

*   *   *

LUKE 11:42

"Woe to you Pharisees, because you give God a tenth of your mint, rue and all other kinds of garden herbs, but you neglect justice and the love of God. You should have practiced the latter without leaving the former undone."

*   *   *

JOHN 15:12-17

"My command is this: Love each other as I have loved you. Greater love has no one than this, that he lay down his life for his friends. You

are my friends if you do what I command. I no longer call you ser-
vants, because a servant does not know his master's business. Instead,
I have called you friends, for everything that I learned from my Father
I have made known to you. You did not choose me, but I chose you
and appointed you to go and bear fruit—fruit that will last. Then the
Father will give you whatever you ask in my name. This is my com-
mand: Love each other."

*   *   *

JAMES 2:1-26

My brothers, as believers in our glorious Lord Jesus Christ, don't show
favoritism. Suppose a man comes into your meeting wearing a gold
ring and fine clothes, and a poor man in shabby clothes also comes in.
If you show special attention to the man wearing fine clothes and say,
"Here's a good seat for you," but say to the poor man, "You stand
there" or "Sit on the floor by my feet," have you not discriminated
among yourselves and become judges with evil thoughts?

Listen, my dear brothers: Has not God chosen those who are poor
in the eyes of the world to be rich in faith and to inherit the kingdom
he promised those who love him? But you have insulted the poor. Is
it not the rich who are exploiting you? Are they not the ones who are
dragging you into court? Are they not the ones who are slandering the
noble name of him to whom you belong?

If you really keep the royal law found in Scripture, "Love your
neighbor as yourself," you are doing right. But if you show favorit-
ism, you sin and are convicted by the law as lawbreakers. For whoever
keeps the whole law and yet stumbles at just one point is guilty of
breaking all of it. For he who said, "Do not commit adultery," also
said, "Do not murder." If you do not commit adultery but do commit
murder, you have become a lawbreaker.

Speak and act as those who are going to be judged by the law that
gives freedom, because judgment without mercy will be shown to any-
one who has not been merciful. Mercy triumphs over judgment!

What good is it, my brothers, if a man claims to have faith but has no deeds? Can such faith save him? Suppose a brother or sister is without clothes and daily food. If one of you says to him, "Go, I wish you well; keep warm and well fed," but does nothing about his physical needs, what good is it? In the same way, faith by itself, if it is not accompanied by action, is dead.

But someone will say, "You have faith; I have deeds."

Show me your faith without deeds, and I will show you my faith by what I do. You believe that there is one God. Good! Even the demons believe that—and shudder.

You foolish man, do you want evidence that faith without deeds is useless? Was not our ancestor Abraham considered righteous for what he did when he offered his son Isaac on the altar? You see that his faith and his actions were working together, and his faith was made complete by what he did. And the scripture was fulfilled that says, "Abraham believed God, and it was credited to him as righteousness," and he was called God's friend. You see that a person is justified by what he does and not by faith alone.

In the same way, was not even Rahab the prostitute considered righteous for what she did when she gave lodging to the spies and sent them off in a different direction? As the body without the spirit is dead, so faith without deeds is dead.

Luke 16:1-13

The Shrewd Manager

UNDERSTANDING THE PARABLE

Jesus told his disciples: "There was a rich man whose manager was accused of wasting his possessions. So he called him in and asked him, 'What is this I hear about you? Give an account of your manage-ment, because you cannot be manager any longer.'

"The manager said to himself, 'What shall I do now? My master is taking away my job. I'm not strong enough to dig, and I'm ashamed to beg— I know what I'll do so that, when I lose my job here, people will welcome me into their houses.'

"So he called in each one of his master's debtors. He asked the first, 'How much do you owe my master?'

" 'Eight hundred gallons of olive oil,' he replied.

"The manager told him, 'Take your bill, sit down quickly, and make it four hundred.'

"Then he asked the second, 'And how much do you owe?'

" 'A thousand bushels of wheat,' he replied.

"He told him, 'Take your bill and make it eight hundred.'

"The master commended the dishonest manager because he had acted shrewdly. For the people of this world are more shrewd in dealing with their own kind than are the people of the light. I tell you, use

worldly wealth to gain friends for yourselves, so that when it is gone, you will be welcomed into eternal dwellings.

"Whoever can be trusted with very little can also be trusted with much, and whoever is dishonest with very little will also be dishonest with much. So if you have not been trustworthy in handling worldly wealth, who will trust you with true riches? And if you have not been trustworthy with someone else's property, who will give you property of your own?

"No servant can serve two masters. Either he will hate the one and love the other, or he will be devoted to the one and despise the other. You cannot serve both God and Money." LUKE 16:1-13

Introduction

The parable of the Shrewd Manager is widely considered one of the most difficult parables — if not *the* most difficult — to understand. It's not hard to see why. A man is charged for wrongdoing and fired by his master; he immediately goes and cheats his master out of more money. Finding out about his loss, his master *praises* the man. Then, even more surprisingly, Jesus tells His disciples that they should be *like* the shrewd manager.

What's going on here?

As with many of the parables, a closer look reveals aspects of the story that could be missed at first. In fact, as we dig deeper, we realize that Jesus has given us an extremely interesting perspective on how God expects us to use our money and resources to further His Kingdom.

The Setting

Jesus told his disciples...

When Jesus told this parable, just who was listening to Him? To answer this we have to turn back a chapter to the beginning of Luke 15. At this point in Jesus' journey toward Jerusalem

"the tax collectors and 'sinners' were all gathering around
to hear him. But the Pharisees and the teachers of the law
muttered, 'This man welcomes sinners and eats with them.'"
(Luke 15:1-2) In light of this mixture of sinners and self-
righteous men before him, Jesus told three parables about
being lost and found: the parables of the lost sheep, the lost
coin, and the lost sons.

Upon finishing, He turned to His own disciples — who
had been standing near Him all along — and told the parable
of the shrewd manager. As soon as He finished that parable,
He gave His own explanation. When the Pharisees heard
this, they laughed at Him. In response, Jesus explained some
facts about the Law, then told the parable of the Rich Man
and Lazarus.

At first glance, these parables — the parables of the lost
things, the parable of the shrewd manager, and the parable
of the Rich Man and Lazarus — may not seem to be related.
But upon deeper inspection there is an unfolding argument
to what Jesus is saying. We will explore His teaching on Luke
15 when we cover the lesson *Prodigal Sons*. For now, however, it
is enough to know that with His first three parables He was in
part addressing the issue of pride, one of the two great sins
that plagued His audience. The second great sin — and one
that some of his disciples likely struggled with as well — was
greed. As many of us well know, the sins of pride and greed
still live with us today in the Church.

Therefore Jesus taught two parables on the topic of money. He first showed what disciples of the Kingdom *should* do
with their financial resources (The Shrewd Manager) and
then what they *should not* do with them (The Rich Man and Lazarus). The bridge between the two parables is Jesus' teaching
in the middle of Luke 16.

We will first look at the parable of the Shrewd Manager to
understand what Jesus was saying with it. In the next chapter we
will explore how Jesus wants us to live in light of it.

An Angry Master

There was a rich man whose manager was accused of wasting his posses-
sions. So he called him in and asked him, 'What is this I hear about you?'
LUKE 16:1-2

Jesus starts His parable by introducing a rich man with a
manager. There were lots of rich men in Jesus' day, and, like
today, it was not unusual for them to have managers who over-
saw their possessions. In this case the possessions the manager was overseeing were agricultural. In other words, he was
a farm manager.

Kenneth Bailey, in examining the cultural setting of
the parable, points out that it paints a picture of "a landed estate with a manager who had the authority to carry
out the business of the estate."[1] It was a large estate, as the
amounts due from the renters signify. Such a large estate
would have had many people other than the manager spending
time on it, people who would naturally notice what the manager
was doing in his day-to-day business.

The master is given a report that his manager has been
wasting his possessions. Just exactly what the waste was, Jesus
does not say. But it was serious enough for the rich man to
realize he was losing money and needed to fire his manager,
not just reprimand him. So the master calls in his manager to
confront him with his wrongdoing.

This is where we pick up our film *The Shrewd Manager*. Jasper
is the farm manager for George Jennings, a wealthy landed
farmer in the Southern tradition. He owns a large farm and
has many renters on his land who all report to Jasper. It is
Jasper's responsibility to take care of Mr. Jennings' property
in his stead.

Jasper, like the manager in the parable, is called in to
see his master. As we saw in the film, the story takes place in

a small farming community. There would have been many similarities between this small town and the village community in Jesus' day. Everyone would have known everyone else. There would have been clear economic differences between the groups of people living in the community, but nevertheless strong relationships. In this case, it is the relationship of a superior to an inferior, and Jasper knows it.

He shows up literally with hat in hand. When confronted with his wrongdoing, he remains strangely silent. When we look back at the original parable, it does not show the manager arguing with his master for his job. Although it seems a bit odd to us, such silence would have spoken volumes to the original Middle Eastern audience. It would have signified that the manager knew he was guilty and that he couldn't get his job back by offering excuses.[2] In a culture where it is normal to defend oneself verbally or to try to hide an offense with words, silence is a full admission of guilt. Just as Jasper realizes he's been caught red-handed, the manager decides it is in his best interest to remain silent and see what happens next.

Fired But Not Jailed — A Gracious Gesture

Give an account of your management, because you cannot be manager any longer. LUKE 16:2

Once the master confirms that the manager is guilty, he immediately tells him to turn in the accounting books.[3] This phrase "give an account of your management" would be understood in the original culture to refer to the records he used to keep track of the accounts under his management. Both the Bible and archaeology demonstrate that agricultural and mercantile records were kept in very accurate detail throughout human history. These books would have been the manager's primary responsibility and, as the story tells, would have been key to understanding the debt relationship between the master and his renters.

At this point the master isn't looking for explanations. He expects obedience and he knows the man is guilty, so he fires him on the spot: "You cannot be manager any longer." Yet there is a note of graciousness even in the midst of his punishment.

It's not what we see the master doing, but what we don't see him do. The original audience would have understood that if a manager was being fired for wastefulness, it meant he had cost the master money, likely through some sort of embezzlement. In light of that, the master had every right to throw the manager in jail.[4]

This is what Mr. Jennings points out to Jasper. He holds Jasper's destiny in his hands, and although Jasper's actions are deserving of legal punishment, Mr. Jennings chooses to overlook that fact and just fire him. Such generosity would not have been overlooked either to the original audience or to the man being fired. There is a sense of mercy that pervades the master's actions, something that will be important to remember at the end of the story.

A Plan Is Shrewdly Formed

The manager said to himself, 'What shall I do now? My master is taking away my job. I'm not strong enough to dig, and I'm ashamed to beg— I know what I'll do so that, when I lose my job here, people will welcome me into their houses.' LUKE 16: 3-4

It doesn't take long for the manager to recognize the gravity of his situation. He immediately starts to cast about to figure out a solution: "What shall I do now?"

This is Jasper's emotional state upon returning to the

backhouse. He starts by recognizing that "Judgment Day has finally come." This idea of impending judgment is implicit to the parable: the manager is out of a job and soon will be without means of sustaining himself. In the world of the parable, he has been judged, but the full punishment has not yet fallen upon him. He must somehow find a way out of his terrible situation.

This brings up an interesting aspect to the parable which Jesus calls out in verse 9: every man is now living under the prospect of judgment and must one day account for his actions on the earth. The sooner man recognizes his situation and works to correct it, the better his situation will turn out. In scholarly circles this is called an *eschatological crisis* ("eschatological" refers to the end times, the word 'eschaton' in Greek meaning 'end'). The recognition that judgment is imminent pushes man toward certain choices and actions.

Of course, in the world of the parable, the consequences aren't nearly so dire – even if they may seem so to both Jasper and the manager. The manager declares that he isn't strong enough to dig (just as Jasper says he couldn't drive a combine), meaning he really isn't suited for manual farm labor. And to say that he's ashamed to beg demonstrates he still has a modicum of pride left – even if he is dishonest.

So he must find a job. Even more than that, since everyone will quickly know he was fired because of wastefulness (and who wants to hire a crook?), he needs a personal makeover in the eyes of the village.[5] In a village community, that's not an easy thing to do. He must somehow find a way to make people want to do something kind for him in his distress. This hope of having people "welcome me into their homes" is his endgame. He needs to do something to make people think he's worth keeping around.

Then it dawns on him. The resources that he has at his disposal can easily be turned to his benefit. This is an important point: he controls everything that can be used to lift himself out of this situation. And because of his master's general graciousness (as evidenced before), perhaps this plan will actually work.

But his window of opportunity is slim. Although he knows he's been fired, and his master knows he's been fired, *no one else knows.* Obviously word will leak out — but because he was fired just minutes before, he knows he has time. This is the key to his plan working; once he turns over the accounting books, he has no hope of changing his situation.[6]

Calling In His New Friends

So he called in each one of his master's debtors. He asked the first, "How much do you owe my master?" "Eight hundred gallons of olive oil," he replied. The manager told him, "Take your bill, sit down quickly, and make it four hundred." Then he asked the second, "And how much do you owe?" "A thousand bushels of wheat," he replied. He told him, "Take your bill and make it eight hundred."
LUKE 16:5-7

Let's spend a few moments looking at just what this debt relationship was between the master and his debtors. It was — and still is — normal for landowners with extensive land holdings to rent out sections of their land to other farmers to farm. Both then and now, the rental price for using the land was normally established at a certain dollar or crop amount before the season began. In many cases, the farmer would agree on assigning a certain amount of his harvest to the landowner as payment for rent.

Note that these rental amounts were established *before* the season began. If it was a particularly dry year or an overly rainy year and the crops didn't produce well, the same amount of rent was still owed to the landowner. However, it would not have been out of the question for a landowner, in light of bad

weather or some other such problem, to make a rental adjust-
ment for his renters to keep them from having to absorb all
the loss. Although it wouldn't happen often, it was certainly
feasible.

These cultural factors would have been assumed by Jesus'
original audience. They also would have understood that the
manager needed to act quickly, for if the renters found out
what he was doing they would never go along with it. Though
such reductions were unusual, the renters would assume they
were authorized by the master.[7]

Yet they would also think it was the manager who had
secured the reductions for them. After all, the whole point of
the manager's plan was to make new friends to prepare for his
future. He would naturally take credit for the reductions since
managing the rent was his responsibility. This assumption is
completely necessary: were the reductions simply the master's
idea, then the manager would be in no better place than he
was at the start.[8] His whole plan hinges on perception, both
his and his master's in the eyes of the community.

After all, this is a small village community. Everyone
knows everyone. And the men who were renters were clearly of
a higher class, as their debts demonstrate. The amounts that
they owe the master (800 gallons of olive oil and 1000 bushels
of wheat) were large amounts. These renters would have been
socially more aligned with the master than with the manager.
As Bailey points out, "The relationship between the owner
of the land and his renters is a significant personal and economic relationship."[9]

In our film, Jasper must work with speed to get the reductions in writing before Mr. Jennings can find out. In the original parable the manager tells the renters to sit down quickly
and write out the difference. This would show the master that
the rent reductions had been completed officially and that the
renters knew of it. Furthermore, the amounts that are reduced are essentially both equal to 500 denarii (the daily wage

for a laborer was one denarius), perhaps demonstrating that the manager was just quickly lopping off the same amount for everyone.[10] Finally, although the parable shows just two renters, a master with land holdings that extensive would have had many more men in his debt, all of whom could have become new friends of the shrewd manager.

A Shrewd Victory

> *The master commended the dishonest manager because he had acted shrewdly.* LUKE 16:8

Thus far, the story has followed a fairly logical plot: a rich man has a farm manager who wasted his property; he calls him in, fires him, and tells him to turn in the books; during a brief window of time, the manager calls in the various renters and drops their rents in order to make them like him.

The manager's next move is to return to the master with the accounting books, per his request. Yet upon his surrendering the books, the master is informed of the discounting that has just gone on under his nose. To a modern audience coming from the cultural West, the next logical step is for the master to become furious, declare that he had been fired and the new rents don't stand, then to throw out the deceptive manager.

But that's not what happens. In a bizarre stroke, the master actually *commends* the dishonest manager because he acted shrewdly. Our film begins to explore the reasons behind this. The master really only has two options: deny the renters their reduction or affirm them. In a world like ours where there are few personal relationships in business, it is easy to deny something to someone you don't know. Yet this is a small village community. And, as we saw in the film, word gets around quickly about what a wonderful, generous man the master is.

The manager has put his master on the horns of a dilemma. As Mr. Jennings says in the film:

If I tell 'em you'd already been fired and they don't get the drop, they ain't gonna like it. If I don't tell 'em and leave it where it is, I ain't gonna like it.

In the East, one of the highest attributes of a nobleman was generosity and graciousness.[11] It was this same quality of mercy that the manager had seen in the master at the start when he was not fully prosecuted for his wrongdoing. Once again, graciousness wins the day.

Although the manager may have made a number of new friends, the master was now considered the hero of the village. And both then and now, wealthy people normally prefer to be known as generous and kind rather than simply wealthy.

And what of the manager? He was complimented for his quick thinking and cleverness. Again, in the Middle East, one of the most valuable traits a person could have was the ability to be shrewd and clever. In this case, Jesus has presented us with a man who is the consummate shrewd character. His shrewdness is seen in four ways:

1   He understood his situation: he was fired, he was not liked, and he had to have a job.
2   He understood his goal: he needed to get people to like him and to want to help him out.
3   He thought about what he had under his control: the accounts, his influence, and his master's renters.
4   He acted quickly to pull all this together into a plan, then executed it.

When looked at from this perspective, it becomes clear that the primary quality which the master appreciates is the manager's *shrewd wisdom.* He has been outfoxed and made to look good in the process: what's a little lost money in the face of so much praise?

The Divine Praise

> *For the people of this world are more shrewd in dealing with their*
> *own kind than are the people of the light. I tell you, use worldly*
> *wealth to gain friends for yourselves, so that when it is gone, you will*
> *be welcomed into eternal dwellings.* LUKE 16:8-9

The puzzling factor of this story is that the praise doesn't end with the master. As verse 8 continues into verse 9, Luke transitions to Jesus' commentary on the parable. It is an interesting commentary, for it doesn't immediately condemn the actions of the manager (which were patently dishonest), but rather holds them up as a pattern for his disciples to emulate.

This is the stumbling point for most people. Yet it shouldn't be. The challenge is understanding exactly the point of comparison that Jesus was making. Thankfully, Jesus provides an in-depth commentary on this parable. He even tells another parable (Luke 16:19-31) to help explain the principle behind the parable of the Shrewd Manager.

Let's look at what Jesus says specifically:

> *For the people of this world are more shrewd in dealing with their*
> *own kind than are the people of the light.*

Jesus is splitting up the world into its two parts: the Kingdom of God (the light) and the kingdom of Satan (this world). He draws a line between the two and then compares them on the basis of their service to their respective kings. He says that the people of the world apply the principles they are supposed to live by with much more wisdom than do the people of God.

The parable is the case in point. The manager, a man of the world, is dishonest at heart. He is unrepentant of his dishonesty even when caught. Instead, when coming to a moment of crisis, he continues to be dishonest and cleverly uses that dishonesty to win more friends within the system of the world. His master, also a man of the world, has to commend the manager for acting shrewdly according to those principles. The manager smartly manipulates his *own kind* — the renters and the master. In the end, he will be rewarded according to the world's system.

And what of the comparison? Remember that Jesus addressed this parable particularly to His disciples (although others were within earshot). His point is simple: you who are children of the Kingdom certainly don't act like you are. Instead of being shrewd according to the principles of the Kingdom and dealing with your own kind as God would command (with generosity, kindness, and love), you are not clever at all. In the moment of crisis, you often miss the point entirely and fail to do what you are supposed to be doing. In this key sense, the people of the world are better at playing their particular game than are the people of the light.

Isn't this the very thing that Christians today so often bemoan? That the church seems woefully incapable of taking care of its own people, much less those who are needy around her?

Many Christians seem much more interested in *going* to church with others than in *being* the church to others. Again, the point of comparison is *not the ethical standard* of the manager but his *proficiency at following the rules of the worldly kingdom.* In Matthew 10:16 Jesus put it another way: be as shrewd as serpents (like the manager in this story), but as innocent as doves (unlike the manager in this story).

Jesus goes on to say pointedly:

> *I tell you, use worldly wealth to gain friends for yourselves, so that when it is gone, you will be welcomed into eternal dwellings.*

This idea of "worldly wealth" is Jesus' way of talking about the money that currently reigns within the world's system.

Although wealth is not a bad thing in itself (remember, God created wealth and some of His favorite people — Abraham, Noah and Job — were quite wealthy), it has often been corrupted by the world and co-opted into one of the great competing idols against God.[12]

Who are the friends Jesus is referring to? Again, by keeping our comparisons straight, if "their own kind" was referring to the people of the world, then the friends Jesus is referring to are those who are highly valued inside the Kingdom. Remember what Jesus said at another time:

> "Then the King will say to those on his right, 'Come, you who are blessed by my Father; take your inheritance, the kingdom prepared for you since the creation of the world. For I was hungry and you gave me something to eat, I was thirsty and you gave me something to drink, I was a stranger and you invited me in, I needed clothes and you clothed me, I was sick and you looked after me, I was in prison and you came to visit me.'
>
> "Then the righteous will answer him, 'Lord, when did we see you hungry and feed you, or thirsty and give you something to drink? When did we see you a stranger and invite you in, or needing clothes and clothe you? When did we see you sick or in prison and go to visit you?'
>
> "The King will reply, 'I tell you the truth, whatever you did for one of the least of these brothers of mine, you did for me.'"
>
> MATT 25:34-40

Notice whom Jesus is interested in being served: "one of the least of these brothers of mine." And many of the things that Jesus lists here require money: food, water, hospitality, clothing, etc.

Wealth that operates according to the principles of this world should be co-opted by disciples of the Kingdom to be used according to the principles of the Kingdom. There is a day when it will be gone — at the end of our own lives or at the end of the world itself. Either way, worldly wealth is passing away and Jesus presses us to recognize the *eschatological crisis* facing each one of us. We are expected to do the works He has "prepared in advance for us to do," more specifically, taking care of those Christians around us who are in need.

Dennis Ireland sums up the point of the parable when he says: "Here Jesus tells his disciples how and why they can practice in their own sphere of existence the wise preparation for the future which the [manager] exercised in his. Jesus says in effect that true wisdom is to use money with eternity in view, 'to use wealth in the service of love.' Unlike the unjust [manager] who at best provided only for his earthly future, acts of charity by disciples will bear interest in eternity."[13]

PARALLELS

ORIGINAL PARABLE	PARABLE FILM
Rich Man – a wealthy farmer.	Mr. Jennings - a wealthy farmer.
Close-knit village community.	Small town.
Manager – overseer of accounts and land.	Jasper – overseer of accounts and land.
Summons manager – sign of authority.	Summons manager – sign of authority.
Hears of wastefulness from unnamed person.	Hears of wastefulness from unnamed person.
Confronts manager with truth.	Confronts manager with truth.
Manager silent – sign of guilt.	Manager silent – sign of guilt.
Fires him – tells him to turn in books.	Fires him – tells him to turn in books.
Does not throw him in jail – a clear sign of the Master's mercy.	Does not turn him into the Sheriff – a clear sign of Mr. Jennings' mercy.

Period of time: he is fired, but no one knows.	Period of time: he is fired, but no one knows.
Manager knows he must act quickly.	Jasper knows he must act quickly.
Manager does not repent even after being fired – he is still dishonest.	Jasper goes and steals Mr. Jennings' lollypops – he is still dishonest.
Manager talks to himself: he is not strong enough to do manual labor.	Jasper talks to his dog, Frank: he is not skilled enough to do manual labor.
Manager is embarrassed to beg.	Jasper is embarrassed to beg.
Manager realizes what he still has at his disposal: his master's assets.	Jasper realizes what he still has at his disposal: Mr. Jennings' assets.
Manager's goal is to make other farmers in the village like him and want to help him once he is out of a job.	Jasper's goal is to make the other farmers in the town like him and want to help him once he is out of his job.
Manager summons Renters (wealthier men) to him – shows he still has authority in their eyes.	Jasper summons wealthier farmers to him – shows he still has authority in their eyes.
Manager moves quickly – he knows he doesn't have much time.	Jasper urges them to move quickly – he knows he doesn't have much time.
Manager ask how much he owes - confirms the amount.	Jasper asks how much he owes – confirms the amount.
Renters owe amounts of produce as payment for use of the Master's land.	Farmers owe amounts of rent as payment for use of Mr. Jennings' land.
Manager removes a large amount from what is owed (approx 500 denarii, or almost 2 years wages of a working man).	Jasper removes a large amount from the rent from what is owed (approx $50,000).

Renters would assume that the master had approved it, otherwise they would not do it.	Farmers assume Mr. Jennings had approved it, otherwise they would not go with it.
Since Manager wanted the Renters to think highly of him, it is natural that he would suggest that he was part of the decision – after all, he was in the fields each day and knew their situation.	Since Jasper wanted the farmers to think highly of him, he suggests that it was his idea after reviewing the Almanac for the year.
The Renters must sign with their own hands – to confirm that they know of the new price.	The Farmers must sign with their own hands – to confirm that they know of the new price.
It would be culturally understood that the Renters would think much more highly both of the Manager and the Master, and would naturally pour out their thanks to both.	The Farmers immediately begin to show their thanks to Jasper, and find ways to show their thanks to Mr. Jennings.
The Master realizes exactly what has happened when he sees the books.	Mr. Jennings realizes exactly what has happened when he sees the books.
There would naturally be social pressure of being honorable on the Master to support the decision of the Manager, even if it cost him money.	There was the social pressure of being honorable on Mr. Jennings to support Jasper's decision, even if it cost him money.
The Master realizes the situation he is in, and is impressed with how shrewd his Manager acted.	Mr. Jennings realizes the situation he is in, and is impressed with how shrewd Jasper is.
The Master shows even more mercy to the Manager in allowing the decision to stand.	Mr. Jennings shows even more mercy to Jasper in allowing the decision to stand.

Endnotes

1   Kenneth Bailey, *Poet and Peasant* (Eerdmans , 1983), 94.

2   Bailey, 97.

3   Bailey, 97.

4   Bailey, 98.

5   Bailey, 98.

6   Bailey, 98-99.

7   Bailey, 100.

8   Bailey, 100.

9   Bailey, 99.

10 Bailey, 101.

11 Bailey, 102.

12 Dennis Ireland, *Stewardship and the Kingdom of God* (Brill, 1992), 99.

13 Ireland, 105.

Luke 16:1-13

The Shrewd Manager
LIVING THE PARABLE

Jesus told his disciples: "There was a rich man whose manager was accused of wasting his possessions. So he called him in and asked him, 'What is this I hear about you? Give an account of your management, because you cannot be manager any longer.'

"The manager said to himself, 'What shall I do now? My master is taking away my job. I'm not strong enough to dig, and I'm ashamed to beg— I know what I'll do so that, when I lose my job here, people will welcome me into their houses.'

"So he called in each one of his master's debtors. He asked the first, 'How much do you owe my master?'

" 'Eight hundred gallons of olive oil,' he replied.

"The manager told him, 'Take your bill, sit down quickly, and make it four hundred.'

"Then he asked the second, 'And how much do you owe?'

" 'A thousand bushels of wheat,' he replied.

"He told him, 'Take your bill and make it eight hundred.'

"The master commended the dishonest manager because he had acted shrewdly. For the people of this world are more shrewd in dealing with their own kind than are the people of the light. I tell you, use

worldly wealth to gain friends for yourselves, so that when it is gone, you will be welcomed into eternal dwellings.

"Whoever can be trusted with very little can also be trusted with much, and whoever is dishonest with very little will also be dishonest with much. So if you have not been trustworthy in handling worldly wealth, who will trust you with true riches? And if you have not been trustworthy with someone else's property, who will give you property of your own?

"No servant can serve two masters. Either he will hate the one and love the other, or he will be devoted to the one and despise the other. You cannot serve both God and Money." LUKE 16:1-13

TRANSCRIPT OF APPLICATION VIDEO

Living out The Shrewd Manager – Dr. Gene Mims

Dr. Gene Mims is Senior Pastor of Judson Baptist Church in Nashville, Tennessee.

Introduction

There are things that strike us as odd at first glance. Things that seem out of place to the casual observer. The parable of the Shrewd Manager is one of those things. It just doesn't seem like the kind of parable that Jesus would tell. And if it *is* a parable He would tell, it seems even more strange that He'd hold up a dishonest man as someone to emulate. What's going on here?

Attacking an Idol

We have a tendency to like to put Jesus in a box and think we understand Him. But the God of the universe won't stay in a box. Even more so, when we look at this parable, we see that He's attacking one of the most common-place idols in our culture or in any culture: the love of money. When it comes down to it, Jesus is telling His disciples that unless they look at all their money and resources in light of how they can be used to advance the Kingdom of God, then they're falling far short of what's expected of them.

Working for Christ

One of the first things Jesus wants to teach us in this parable is that we are all working for Him. He has inaugurated His Kingdom, He has given His Holy Spirit, and He has sent us out, His disciples, to do His work of advancing His Kingdom.

But a number of us have squandered what He's given us on ourselves. We've essentially embezzled His blessings for our own uses. He's given us money, he's given us resources, and what are we doing with them? Jesus is using this parable to remind His disciples that they are ultimately accountable to Him.

Many Christians don't think that they will be judged by Christ for their actions in this life. But the Bible is very clear: Christ will judge His own according to how they followed His commands. We have duties that are expected of us. We should be setting our goals for the advancement of the Kingdom. And we should be discerning as to how to use the money and resources that have been given to us.

Although we may not think about it often, Christ expects us to work for Him on a daily basis. And for those of us who have been given resources and are squandering them, we should remember that judgment can come suddenly and unexpectedly.

Our Money in His Service

So what are we to do? Jesus was using this parable as a wake-up call for His disciples. As good teachers often do, Jesus used an ironic sense of humor to drive home His point — but the truth behind the humor is hard and challenging.

We must first realize our situation: Jesus has made it our duty to use our money toward building up His Kingdom. It is not our money, but His — and He expects us to use it in His service.

How are we to use it? Shrewdly. That is the operative word. The point of comparison between the disciples and the shrewd manager is not his dishonesty — Jesus condemns dishonest servants just a few verses later. Rather, it is the manager's shrewdness in using what His master has put at His disposal that matters.

Just as the shrewd manager used His master's money to make friends for Himself (and to make His master look good in the process), so too are we to use the money that the Lord has given us to make friends for ourselves (and to make the Lord look good in the process). This is what Jesus Himself says in Luke 16:9 - "I tell you, use worldly wealth to gain friends for yourselves, so that when it is gone, you will be welcomed into eternal dwellings."

How We Are to Treat Our Friends

But who are those friends? In the parable it's those who are debtors to the manager's master. But in real life, Jesus tells us that we are to be using our money and resources to be helping those brothers and sisters of the Kingdom who are in need around us. Remember that the parable of the Shrewd Manager is followed by the parable of the Rich Man and Lazarus. The first is an example of what we should be doing with our money; the second is an example of what happens to those who ignore God's commands.

Let's remember what Jesus tells His disciples in Matthew 25: "Then the King will say to those on His right, 'Come, you who are blessed by my Father; take your inheritance, the kingdom prepared for you since the creation of the world. For I was hungry and you gave me something to eat, I was thirsty and you gave me something to drink, I was a stranger and you invited me in, I needed clothes and you clothed me, I was sick and you looked after me, I was in prison and you came to visit me.'" He then says, "I tell you the truth, whatever you did for one of the least of these brothers of mine, you did for me." It is our duty to be using Kingdom resources to take care of the children of the Kingdom.

Yet it doesn't stop there. This parable should cause us to rethink our goals with our money. The fact is, many of us spend much more time thinking about how we can use our money for our own betterment than we do in bettering the Kingdom. Jesus expected this and He warned us that "No servant can serve two masters. Either he will hate the one and love the other, or he will be devoted to the one and despise the other. You cannot serve both God and Money."

Who is Our True Master?

We have heard this said many times, yet in our current culture we have softened it to avoid the real rub: who is our true master?

Here is where we must strive for Biblical discernment. Where are we spending our money and resources? Just open your checkbook or look at your credit card receipt: where is your money going? It is said that many in the church don't give the ten percent tithe that is required of them, much less think shrewdly about how they can use their money to further the Kingdom. Search your heart — what would Jesus say to you about the way you use your money? Are you being shrewd with it in terms of the Kingdom?

It is not surprising that Jesus used a dishonest, worldly man to teach His disciples about using money: for as He Himself says, the people of this world are more shrewd in their use of money and dealing with their own kind than we are in using money and building up the Kingdom.

Look at the entrepreneurial spirit of those outside the Kingdom: they think constantly about how to make more money and elevate themselves; they go to school to learn this; they read books; they work long hours. After all, they know the reward that will come to them in this life.

But what about us? Have we forgotten the rewards that will come to us in the life to come? If we are shrewd with our money today, in light of the Kingdom of God, then we will certainly be welcomed into the eternal dwellings when this world passes away.

ADDITIONAL VERSES FOR STUDY AND REFLECTION

LUKE 16:15A, 19-31

[Jesus] said to them,... "There was a rich man who was dressed in purple and fine linen and lived in luxury every day. At his gate was laid a beggar named Lazarus, covered with sores and longing to eat what fell from the rich man's table. Even the dogs came and licked his sores.

"The time came when the beggar died and the angels carried him to Abraham's side. The rich man also died and was buried. In hell, where he was in torment, he looked up and saw Abraham far away, with Lazarus by his side. So he called to him, 'Father Abraham, have pity on me and send Lazarus to dip the tip of his finger in water and cool my tongue, because I am in agony in this fire.'

"But Abraham replied, 'Son, remember that in your lifetime you received your good things, while Lazarus received bad things, but now he is comforted here and you are in agony. And besides all this, between us and you a great chasm has been fixed, so that those who want to go from here to you cannot, nor can anyone cross over from there to us.'

"He answered, 'Then I beg you, father, send Lazarus to my father's house, for I have five brothers. Let him warn them, so that they will not also come to this place of torment.'

"Abraham replied, 'They have Moses and the Prophets; let them listen to them.'

" 'No, father Abraham,' he said, 'but if someone from the dead goes to them, they will repent.'

"He said to him, 'If they do not listen to Moses and the Prophets, they will not be convinced even if someone rises from the dead.'"

*   *   *

ACTS 5:1-11

Now a man named Ananias, together with his wife Sapphira, also sold a piece of property. With his wife's full knowledge he kept back part of the money for himself, but brought the rest and put it at the apostles' feet.

Then Peter said, "Ananias, how is it that Satan has so filled your heart that you have lied to the Holy Spirit and have kept for yourself some of the money you received for the land? Didn't it belong to you before it was sold? And after it was sold, wasn't the money at your disposal? What made you think of doing such a thing? You have not lied to men but to God."

When Ananias heard this, he fell down and died. And great fear seized all who heard what had happened. Then the young men came forward, wrapped up his body, and carried him out and buried him.

About three hours later his wife came in, not knowing what had happened. Peter asked her, "Tell me, is this the price you and Ananias got for the land?"

"Yes," she said, "that is the price."

Peter said to her, "How could you agree to test the Spirit of the Lord? Look! The feet of the men who buried your husband are at the door, and they will carry you out also."

At that moment she fell down at his feet and died. Then the young men came in and, finding her dead, carried her out and buried her beside her husband. Great fear seized the whole church and all who heard about these events.

*   *   *

1 TIMOTHY 6:6-11

But godliness with contentment is great gain. For we brought noth-ing into the world, and we can take nothing out of it. But if we have food and clothing, we will be content with that. People who want to get rich fall into temptation and a trap and into many foolish and harmful desires that plunge men into ruin and destruction. For the love of money is a root of all kinds of evil. Some people, eager for money, have wandered from the faith and pierced themselves with many griefs.

But you, man of God, flee from all this, and pursue righteousness, godliness, faith, love, endurance and gentleness.

*   *   *

1 Corinthians 16:1-3

Now about the collection for God's people: Do what I told the Galatian churches to do. On the first day of every week, each one of you should set aside a sum of money in keeping with his income, saving it up, so that when I come no collections will have to be made. Then, when I arrive, I will give letters of introduction to the men you approve and send them with your gift to Jerusalem.

*   *   *

Nehemiah 1:1-2:8

The words of Nehemiah son of Hacaliah:

In the month of Kislev in the twentieth year, while I was in the citadel of Susa, Hanani, one of my brothers, came from Judah with some other men, and I questioned them about the Jewish remnant that survived the exile, and also about Jerusalem.

They said to me, "Those who survived the exile and are back in the province are in great trouble and disgrace. The wall of Jerusalem is broken down, and its gates have been burned with fire."

When I heard these things, I sat down and wept. For some days I mourned and fasted and prayed before the God of heaven. Then I said:

"O LORD, God of heaven, the great and awesome God, who
keeps his covenant of love with those who love him and obey his commands, let your ear be attentive and your eyes open to hear the prayer
your servant is praying before you day and night for your servants, the
people of Israel. I confess the sins we Israelites, including myself and
my father's house, have committed against you. We have acted very
wickedly toward you. We have not obeyed the commands, decrees and
laws you gave your servant Moses.

"Remember the instruction you gave your servant Moses, saying,
'If you are unfaithful, I will scatter you among the nations, but if you
return to me and obey my commands, then even if your exiled people
are at the farthest horizon, I will gather them from there and bring
them to the place I have chosen as a dwelling for my Name.'

"They are your servants and your people, whom you redeemed by
your great strength and your mighty hand. O Lord, let your ear be
attentive to the prayer of this your servant and to the prayer of your
servants who delight in revering your name. Give your servant success
today by granting him favor in the presence of this man."

I was cupbearer to the king.

In the month of Nisan in the twentieth year of King Artaxerxes,
when wine was brought for him, I took the wine and gave it to the
king. I had not been sad in his presence before; so the king asked me,
"Why does your face look so sad when you are not ill? This can be
nothing but sadness of heart."

I was very much afraid, but I said to the king, "May the king live forever! Why should my face not look sad when the city where my fathers
are buried lies in ruins, and its gates have been destroyed by fire?"

The king said to me, "What is it you want?"

Then I prayed to the God of heaven, and I answered the king, "If
it pleases the king and if your servant has found favor in his sight, let
him send me to the city in Judah where my fathers are buried so that I
can rebuild it."

Then the king, with the queen sitting beside him, asked me, "How
long will your journey take, and when will you get back?" It pleased
the king to send me; so I set a time.

Luke 18:1-8

LESSON SEVEN
The Widow and Judge
UNDERSTANDING THE PARABLE

Then Jesus told his disciples a parable to show them that they should always pray and not give up. He said: "In a certain town there was a judge who neither feared God nor cared about men. And there was a widow in that town who kept coming to him with the plea, 'Grant me justice against my adversary.'

"For some time he refused. But finally he said to himself, 'Even though I don't fear God or care about men, yet because this widow keeps bothering me, I will see that she gets justice, so that she won't eventually wear me out with her coming!'"

And the Lord said, "Listen to what the unjust judge says. And will not God bring about justice for his chosen ones, who cry out to him day and night? Will he keep putting them off? I tell you, he will see that they get justice, and quickly. However, when the Son of Man comes, will he find faith on the earth?" LUKE 18:1-8

Introduction

Widows occupy an interesting place in the Bible. Since almost all ancient societies were set up as patriarchies, women needed to be joined to men in marriage in order to be provided for and protected. Hebrew society was no different in this respect. When a woman lost a husband, it was normal for her to re-marry quickly, assuming she was young enough for re-marriage to be possible. The book of Ruth reveals it was easy for Ruth to re-marry, but impossible for Naomi. Naomi needed someone like Ruth to take care of her on a daily basis.

But there was not always someone like Ruth to take care of widows. As a result, widows were one of the most overlooked and potentially oppressed groups in ancient society. Widows were normally poor, older women. Because they had lost their husbands, they often did not have an easy way to provide for themselves. Furthermore, what they did have in terms of land or possessions was easy prey for others to exploit since, lacking a husband, a widow had no one to protect her.

Into this world of weakness and oppression God consistently speaks hope. When He handed down His law in Exodus and Deuteronomy, He gave clear instructions concerning widows: "Do not take advantage of a widow or an orphan." (Ex 22:22); "[God] defends the cause of the fatherless and the widow..." (Deut 10:18); and "Cursed is the man who withholds justice from the alien, the fatherless or the widow." (Deut 27:19) God understood that it is the weak in society who need the most care, so He took a personal interest in their protection and well-being. It is for this reason that Jesus chose the widow as the perfect example for teaching His disciples to be persistent in prayer.

The Setting and Context

Then Jesus told his disciples a parable to show them that they should always pray and not give up. LUKE 18:1

Once again we see that Jesus is directing a parable toward His disciples to teach them a lesson. At this point in Luke, Jesus is on His journey to Jerusalem to face crucifixion and death. The parable of the Widow and Judge comes at the end of a series of teachings by Jesus that begins in Luke 17:20 when the Pharisees ask Him when the Kingdom of God will come. They wouldn't find it by looking for it, Jesus answers— at least not the way they had been been looking for it. "The Kingdom of God is within you [or among you, or in your midst]." (Lk 17:21)

He then turns to His disciples and explains some of the things that will mark His next coming. There will be a period when His disciples "will long to see one of the days of the Son of Man" but they will not see it. To clarify the significance of this period of waiting and struggle before the coming judgment, Jesus goes on to make two historical comparisons. This period would be like "the days of Noah" and "the days of Lot." Noah prepared for the flood while the people of his day lived oblivious to the judgment that would soon come. Similarly, Lot kept his faith in God while his neighbors in Sodom ignored God's coming judgment. In both cases, Jesus says judgment came suddenly on those unprepared, sinful people while Noah and Lot were saved.

Why were they saved? The author of Hebrews tells us that in the case of Noah it was as a result of his *faith*. (Heb 11:17) And although the Bible says nothing about Lot in this regard, we have to assume that he had faith left within him, especially in light of the way Jesus uses him in this comparison.

So what does that mean for our parable? When Jesus tells the parable of the Widow and Judge to the disciples, He is assuming that there will be a long period in which His disciples will struggle as they wait and prepare for His coming. It is a period in which they will likely be oppressed by the people who live and act as if there is no judgment coming and no Kingdom of God. In fact, His teaching from Luke 17:20-37 could have left the disciples with a sense of fear and trepidation: what were they going to do during those days when they longed to see the Son of Man, but He was not appearing? Even more so, what recourse did they have when they were oppressed and trodden down by the people of the world?

In response to this concern, Jesus "told his disciples a parable to show them that they should always pray and not give up." Prayer was the answer to their problems, and both the parable and Jesus' commentary afterward explain why.

A Damnable Judge

In a certain town there was a judge who neither feared God nor cared about men. LUKE 18:2

If ancient society placed widows at the bottom of the social scale, then judges were near the top. As the designated interpreters of the law, judges were key to the successful operation of society, both then and now. God provides a special place for judges in Hebrew life telling the Israelites to "appoint judges and officials for each of your tribes in every town the LORD your God is giving you, and they shall judge the people fairly. Do not pervert justice or show partiality. Do not accept a bribe, for a bribe blinds the eyes of the wise and twists the words of the righteous." (Deut 16:18-19)

Just as God knew that widows could easily be oppressed and took steps to protect them, He also knew that the power and influence possessed by judges could lead to their dishonesty and made it clear how they should judge the people. Nevertheless, it was not uncommon to find dishonest judges throughout Israel's history. Both the Old Testament and non-Biblical records talk of dishonest judges ruling in the land. In light of that, Jesus painted a picture of a judge who is so corrupt that he has denied the two essential relationships his office is dedicated to uphold: his relationship with God and his relationship with man.

To begin with, a judge was expected to interpret God's law

faithfully. In this respect, he had to *fear* or *respect* God's law as the highest standard in society. But this judge clearly has no respect for God Himself; and if he doesn't respect God, he certainly cares little for accurately interpreting His law.

As to the second point, the whole purpose of having judges was to "judge the people fairly." Judges were established in order to take care of the people and protect them from injustice. But if this judge doesn't care about mankind, then he certainly isn't worried about being fair or bringing justice to the people. The only person he cares about is himself.

This is the type of judge that we find in our film. Judge Roy Branscomb enters the story yelling at an innocent woman and continues to elevate himself over everyone, regardless of his or her place in society. He knows he runs the town and that there is nothing anyone can do to him. In our society, he is a contradiction of what we think a proper judge should be. There is a natural tendency for us to recoil at such a perversion of the judicial office.

Jesus wanted His listeners to feel the same shock and disgust we feel at the sight of a judge railing against an old lady trying to cross the street. At the center of His parable is a character who is the *exact opposite* of what a judge should be. He is the perfect model of ungodly behavior. And into his court – one that is no doubt marked with corruption and inefficiency – comes a poor widow desperately needing help.

A Desperate Widow

> And there was a widow in that town who kept coming to him with the plea, "Grant me justice against my adversary." LUKE 18:3

We briefly discussed the unique position widows occupy in the Bible. God's law addressed the widow's needs and made provision for her in Hebrew society. Nevertheless, the widow was often abused and unprotected, especially when the times became idolatrous.

As a result, the widow, although a real historical figure, also became a symbol for the weak and humble in society.[1] When someone was particularly evil, they would be known to "take the widow's ox in pledge" or "slay the widow." (Job 24:21; Ps 94:6) In contrast to this, God became the protector of the widow: "a defender of widows, is God in his holy dwelling" and "The LORD...sustains...the widow, but he frustrates the ways of the wicked." (Ps 68:5; Ps 146:9)

As a symbol of all that was weak and needed taking care of, the disciples would have understood the Biblical precedent for judges taking care of widows. They would have known that widows needed justice and protection applied to them, particularly because of their vulnerable situation.

In our film these parallels have been recreated in a small Southern town. Although many things have changed in our country since the passage of Civil Rights legislation in the 1960's, there is still the sense that older African-Americans in a Southern town are symbols of racial oppression. Our widow is Hannah Jackson. Her race, age, and financial situation clearly put her at a disadvantage in the judicial realm of a corrupt judge. Just as an old Hebrew widow would have had little influence in a corrupt court, so too does Hannah have little influence over Judge Branscomb.

The disciples implicitly understood that this situation was wrong on numerous counts, just as we implicitly comprehend its injustice. To the first-century Jew, if anyone should be treated with respect and justice, it was a widow; to us, if anyone should be treated with respect and justice, it is an older African-American woman. The fact that both have historically been denied justice when they needed it makes their circumstances that much more significant.

But what was the nature of the justice this widow needed?

There are two types of justice found in the Bible.[2] We are very familiar with the first: *retributive justice*. This is the justice that we normally associate with 'giving someone their due.' It consists of negative judgment and punishment of the guilty. In this type of justice, God "is coming out of his dwelling to punish the people of the earth for their sins." (Is 26:21)

And yet there is another type of justice found in the Bible with which we are perhaps less familiar, but which is much more important to us: *restorative justice*. This is the type of justice we associate with 'being given what we need.' It consists of positive justice and the uplifting of the weak or oppressed. In restorative justice, God "works righteousness and justice for all the oppressed" and "with righteousness he will judge the needy, with justice he will give decisions for the poor of the earth." (Ps 103:6; Is 11:4)

It is restorative justice that the widow is seeking. She is in great need, no one is taking up her cause, and so she must appeal to this judge to restore what is rightfully hers.

What exactly is the nature of her request? A number of scholars have argued that the situation has to do with money or land or something else of financial value, primarily because that was one of the only things widows might have that someone else would want.[3] In our film, Hannah has had her house destroyed and the perpetrator does not want to pay for it. Although the judge may recognize her right in the case, he is completely uninterested in helping her out.

A Delay of Judgment

For some time he refused. LUKE 18:4

The Old Testament and extra-Biblical records show us that corrupt judges often required bribes or "fees" from those who hoped to navigate their judicial system.[4] (Is 1:23) This was the natural offshoot of denying God's law; God himself anticipated this result of judicial sin and specifically told judges not to accept bribes (Deut 16:19). Although the text does not explicitly state that this judge took bribes, it is a logical presumption to make in light of the historical situation.[5]

Such a requirement would only add an additional financial burden onto the widow, something she naturally could not afford. In our film, the judge has created a sham "donation" system which people pay into in order to have their cases heard or cleared. But this is of no use to Hannah.

The situation before the widow is bleak: as a widow, she would normally be one of the first cases to be heard, but the judge disregards God's law; as an unprotected woman, she would normally be one of the first people to be cared for, but the judge cares nothing about people. What recourse does she have?

Jesus' parable tells us that "for some time he refused." What was the widow doing during this time? Jesus gives us a clue to this in verse 7 when He talks about His chosen ones crying out to God day and night. In the ancient world, a widow could cry out to a judge to give her justice without having to worry about someone throwing her out. As a woman, she would have been out of place in court (it was a man's domain), but as a woman, no one could physically touch her or make her leave, so long as she was just crying out to the judge.[6]

This is what the widow does: she cries out and cries out, her high-pitched voice likely rising above the throng of men gathering around the judge. It is a frustrating and painful affair for her. The judge would have had no reason to answer her cry and could simply ignore her. During this period of struggle and waiting, so far as she could tell, the judge was not going to give her justice. Shouldn't she just give up?

But she has one thing working in her favor: *persistence.* This is the quality that Jesus wants His disciples to notice. In the face of impossible odds the widow continues to cry out for justice. And although he refuses for some time, her persistent crying begins to wear on him.

The Judge's Response

But finally he said to himself, "Even though I don't fear God or care about men, yet because this widow keeps bothering me, I will see that she gets justice, so that she won't eventually wear me out with her coming!" LUKE 18:5

Although Jesus started the parable on a dark note, he ends it with an ironic touch of humor. It is amusing that the judge recognizes his own corruption. He flatly states that he does not answer to God or man — so why is he giving her justice? Because her crying out is bothering him! He is concerned far more about his own sanity and welfare than he is hers, another ironic point that shows the depth of his corruption.

A number of commentators have noted the interesting language the judge uses to refer to what she is doing to him. In the Greek, the verb translated here as "wear out" means "to blacken the eye" or to beat unmercifully.[7] In other words, the widow's persistent crying out has metaphorically beaten him down as a boxer would an opponent, and he is tired of taking so many blows to the head. The widow has found his weak side and mercilessly exploits it.

This is the situation we see in our film. Hannah realizes that the only thing she can control is her own persistence. As many old sayings wisely teach, you can't win if you stop trying. The story takes on a lighter note as we realize that Hannah is getting under the judge's skin and there's nothing he can do about it.

In the end, the judge decides to grant her justice. The poor, helpless, oppressed widow has won a complete victory over the rich, strong, domineering judge.

Jesus' Commentary on the Parable

And the Lord said, "Listen to what the unjust judge says. And will not God bring about justice for his chosen ones, who cry out to him day and night? Will he keep putting them off? I tell you, he will see that they get justice, and quickly. However, when the Son of Man comes, will he find faith on the earth?" LUKE 18:6-8

As we have seen with other parables, Jesus draws a strong comparison between the world of the parable and the spiritual world He is trying to explain. In this case, He is comparing the unjust, corrupt judge to God himself: "Listen to what the unjust judge says. And will not God..." What an ironic comparison!

Jesus sometimes used a technique of taking an example and arguing from its extreme opposite in order to highlight the differences between the two. It is as if He is saying, "if what is bad can do a good thing, then what is good will certainly do a much, much better thing." For example, notice what Jesus says in a parallel passage on prayer: "Which of you fathers, if your son asks for a fish, will give him a snake instead? Or if he asks for an egg, will give him a scorpion? If you then, though you are evil, know how to give good gifts to your children, how much more will your Father in heaven give the Holy Spirit to those who ask him!" (Luke 11:11-13)

This is the line of reasoning Jesus is making with this parable: if an unjust and evil judge will do what's right when pressured, how much more will the holy and just Judge of the universe do what's right when it's requested of Him? To push the comparison further, where the unjust judge completely disregards God's law, God Himself upholds His law perfectly; where the unjust judge cares nothing for other people, God Himself loves his children with an eternal love; and where the unjust judge begrudgingly gives justice in a self-serving manner, God Himself lovingly gives justice in a selfless manner.

After all, Jesus knew that those living in His Kingdom would (and will) face difficult times and be oppressed by the world while they waited for His coming. But just as the persistence of Noah and Lot were ultimately vindicated by God's judgment, so too will the disciples be vindicated by Christ's coming. The issue that faced them, and which faces us now, is *how to persevere* in the interim.

Which brings us to the widow. If the unjust judge is being compared to God, then the widow is being compared to the children of the Kingdom. Again, in an argument from an extreme example to what is true, where the widow is helpless and has no one to defend her, those in the Kingdom are defended by God Himself; where the widow has no husband, those in the Kingdom are married to Christ through the Church; and where the widow does not know if the judge will ever give her justice, those in the Kingdom can be fully assured that God will give them the justice they cry out for. It is as if Jesus is saying, "If the widow who is the picture of weakness can persevere, how much more you who are the children of God?"

This is what Jesus is reminding His disciples when He asks, "will not God bring about justice for his *chosen ones*?" God has an eternal interest in the disciples of the Kingdom, since He has chosen them for salvation. Paul shows us the thinking behind the word 'chosen' when he says in Ephesians: "In him we were also *chosen*, having been predestined according to the plan of him who works out everything in conformity with the purpose of his will, in order that we, who were the first to hope in Christ, might be for the praise of his glory." (Eph 1:11-12)

In other words, those who are in Christ's Kingdom are being prepared by God for His ultimate glory. There is a strong love relationship between God and His chosen ones. As a result, it is ridiculous to think that He would treat them as if He were an unjust judge. He knows His people, living in a fallen world, often struggle with problems that oppress them, but their cries are not being ignored. We can be sure that Christ is returning one day, and during the interim we must not give up in our communication with God. Although it may appear to be hopeless, it is only because we are looking at the details and missing the bigger picture.

And how does prayer fit into that picture? Prayer has everything to do with the power of the Holy Spirit. As Jesus told us in Luke 11:13 when ending His discussion on prayer, God gives the Holy Spirit to those who ask Him. And it is Christ working through the Holy Spirit who ensures that restorative justice is done to those in need. Listen to what God says in Isaiah on this subject:

> *"Here is my servant, whom I uphold, my chosen one in whom*
> *I delight;*
> *I will put my Spirit on him and he will bring justice to the nations.*
> *He will not shout or cry out, or raise his voice in the streets.*
> *A bruised reed he will not break, and a smoldering wick he will not*
> *snuff out.*
> *In faithfulness he will bring forth justice; he will not falter or be*
> *discouraged till he establishes justice on earth. "*
>
> ISAIAH 42:1-4

A bruised reed is a plant whose stem has been broken and hangs down, but has not been snapped off; a smoldering wick is a candle that has burned down, but not gone out completely. Both of these images stand for men and women who have been so oppressed by evil that they are almost gone, but instead of breaking off the reed or snuffing out the wick, Jesus comes beside them and *restores* them with true justice; He brings them life, righteousness, and hope.

Prayer, therefore, is direct communication with the true Judge. He is a Judge who cares for the oppressed and desires to answer their prayers when they bring them to Him. And even if it appears as if He is delaying His answer, and even if times are difficult, Jesus tells His disciples that they must persevere in faith *because God will quickly bring them justice*.

But what does "quickly" refer to? After all, the judge in the parable does not move quickly. For those of us who are praying and seeking God's Kingdom, it may often appear that He is not moving quickly. In fact, we might have prayed for years for justice in a matter that we feel strongly about, and the Lord does not seem to have answered it at all.

This is where we must have faith like Noah and Lot. Jesus is telling us that even though the circumstances may scream the opposite, the fact is that He is returning one day; and because of this fact, God is listening to our prayers and quickly working toward answering them *according to His will*. That is what we have to remember. As Peter tells us: "Do not forget this one thing, dear friends: With the Lord a day is like a thousand years, and a thousand years are like a day. The Lord is not slow in keeping his promise, as some understand slowness. He is patient with you, not wanting anyone to perish, but everyone to come to repentance." (2 Pet 3:8-9)

Jesus recognizes that it will be painful during this interim period. Yet He has not left us like widows but has given us His Holy Spirit to support us through these long days of the Kingdom's growth and struggle. The Holy Spirit ensures that there will be faith on the earth when Jesus returns. That is the answer to His rhetorical question: *When the Son of Man comes, will he find faith on the earth?* Because of the Holy Spirit, the answer is, yes, He will. On an individual basis, however, we must appropriate that faith for ourselves and pray with perseverance that Christ's Kingdom will grow and lead to His soon return. This is, after all, what He has taught us to pray:

> *Our Father in heaven, hallowed be your name,*
> *your kingdom come, your will be done on earth as it is in heaven.*
> MATT 6:9-10

PARALLELS

ORIGINAL PARABLE	PARABLE FILM
Set in a village.	Set in a small Southern town.
A judge whose responsibility is to provide justice for people.	A judge whose responsibility is to provide justice for people.
The judge does not fear God.	The judge says he doesn't care if the man waiting at the top of the stairs worked "for God almighty himself."
The judge does not care about men.	The judge shows respect for no one besides himself.
A widow.	A widow, Hannah Jackson.
In Biblical times, an old widow was often helpless, even to the point of being oppressed.	Even in recent times, some older African-American women are helpless, even to the point of being oppressed.
The widow had been the victim of an injustice, likely financial.	Hannah had been the victim of an injustice, clearly financial.
A widow would have been poor.	Hannah is poor.
Comes to him with a plea.	Brings her case to the court as she knows best.
Likely cried out to him every day, as would have been allowed in a middle eastern court.	Came every day and even approached him, as is the custom in modern courts.
The case was likely a situation of a wealthy person exploiting her helpless state, and either taking something from her or not allowing her to have what was hers (such as rent).	The case is a situation of a wealthy landowner exploiting Hannah's helpless state, and not wanting to pay for her house.

The widow wants the judge to "grant her justice."	Hannah wants the judge to take up her case and decide in her favor.
The judge is clearly corrupt, most likely taking "fees" (or bribes) on the side in order to even hear a case.	The judge is corrupt, having set up a means of taking bribes through "donations to the courthouse."
The judge is not moved by mercy or compassion to help.	The judge is not moved by mercy or compassion to help.
For some time he refused.	Hannah must wait a number of days for her case to be heard.
He realizes that she is not going anywhere and her continual presence is causing him a headache.	He realizes that she is going to wait him out and her presence is bothering him greatly.
He decides to give her justice so that she will go away.	He decides to hear her case so that she will go away.
He finds the case in her favor, otherwise she would just come back.	He will find the case in her favor, otherwise she would just bother him more.

Endnotes

1 Kenneth Bailey, *Poet & Peasant* (Eerdmanns, 1983), 133.
2 Joe Novenson, sermon on Luke 16:1-15, May 6, 2007.
3 Bailey, 133.
4 Bailey, 133.
5 Craig Blomberg, *Preaching the Parables* (Baker, 2004), 174.
6 Bailey, 134.
7 Arland J. Hultgren, *The Parables of Jesus* (Eerdmans, 2002), 255.

Luke 18:1-8

The Widow and Judge

LIVING THE PARABLE

Then Jesus told his disciples a parable to show them that they should always pray and not give up. He said: "In a certain town there was a judge who neither feared God nor cared about men. And there was a widow in that town who kept coming to him with the plea, 'Grant me justice against my adversary.'

"For some time he refused. But finally he said to himself, 'Even though I don't fear God or care about men, yet because this widow keeps bothering me, I will see that she gets justice, so that she won't eventually wear me out with her coming!'"

And the Lord said, "Listen to what the unjust judge says. And will not God bring about justice for his chosen ones, who cry out to him day and night? Will he keep putting them off? I tell you, he will see that they get justice, and quickly. However, when the Son of Man comes, will he find faith on the earth?" LUKE 18:1-8

TRANSCRIPT OF
APPLICATION VIDEO

Living out The Widow and Judge —
Dr. George Grant

Dr. George Grant is Senior Pastor of Parish Presbyterian Church in Franklin, Tennessee.

Introduction

Most Christians, if they're really honest, know that their prayer lives just aren't what they ought to be. They know that they ought to pray more. They know that they should probably have more intimacy in their relationship with the Lord. And, for the most part, they are likely to be frustrated by that—perhaps even feeling guilty. That may be the case with you.

Maybe it's because of the pace of our lives. The tyranny of the urgent and the day-to-day responsibilities tend to push prayer to the margins of our lives. As a result, you know that your prayer life is not all that you would want it to be. It's not all that it should be.

Maybe it's the case that you have been praying—maybe even praying for a long time, but are frustrated with the results. Some of us have serious problems facing us. We have been praying for a long time, but there doesn't seem to be a ready answer.

It should comfort us to know that Jesus understood this struggle. He understood that those living in His Kingdom would face many difficulties in this life, and He told this parable—the parable of the Widow and Judge—to encourage us in the midst of those struggles.

A Judicial Comparison

Unlike some of Jesus' other parables, this one is not actually a comparison of very similar things. Instead, it's a comparison of two completely opposite things. The unjust judge is a man filled with anger and indifference. He is compared to the Judge of the Universe, a God filled with compassion and love.

One judge treats the struggling and the needy with complete contempt, ignoring wrongs that have been done to them and even heaping more wrongs upon them. The other Judge seeks out the struggling and the needy, understands just what wrongs have been done, and then gives them true justice—setting the wrongs right.

The question is, "Why would Jesus compare a corrupt judge with the Glorious King of the Universe?" And what does that mean for us?

It's important to remember what Jesus was talking about just before He told this parable. He had been reminding His disciples of the difficulties facing Noah and Lot in the interim before God's Judgment came. Jesus implied that His disciples would have to endure very similar difficulties before the final Judgment.

Then He told them this parable to encourage them to keep praying in spite of all the outward difficulties. He had told them to pray many times before; in fact, the Old Testament law had established it as one of man's chief duties to pray regularly. But Jesus knew that it would be difficult for His disciples more often than not.

Yet the question still remains: why would Jesus choose an unjust judge as a point of comparison? Is it possible that Jesus thought that some people might actually view God as a capricious, unfeeling ruler who only dispensed justice to the best, to the brightest, and the most influential people? Could He have been playing on the assumption that some people have subconsciously made about God throughout the centuries as a result of their sin?

The fact is many people *have* viewed God in that way and many people still do. Is that true of us? A quick way to measure how we really see God is to look at our interaction with Him in terms of how He answers our prayers. When we do pray, do we believe that we are coming to a loving Father who has our best interests at heart? Or an unjust judge who couldn't care less about us?

Our View of Prayer Relates to Our View of God

Prayer is such an internal relationship, such a key part of our personal experience with God. It is a communion that should be marked by warmth, understanding, and intimacy. Is that true of you? Your communion with God really reflects your personal views of Him. I'm not referring to what you may *say* about God, but what you really *think*. Our thoughts are always seen best in our actions. And because prayer is spiritual—what the ancient Christians called "the breathing of the soul"—it's something that we really can't see easily in others.

But we sure can tell when it's lacking. We can see it in the fear that sets in, the frustration, the worry. These are all the natural results of believing God isn't really good, that He isn't really loving. Rather, (in those circumstances) He seems to us to be like (or perhaps really is) the unjust judge. That is exactly how you will treat Him in prayer. You will grow weary. You will stop praying. You will lose faith.

The Nature of the True Judge

Then Jesus reminds us that the true Judge of the Universe is not like that at all. Jesus knew well of whom He was talking because Jesus was Himself, and is even now, that Judge. We see Him described in the Old Testament in the Prophet Isaiah, where the Father says:

"My servant, whom I uphold, my chosen one in whom I delight – "

Now remember that word "chosen." He continues saying:

"I will put my spirit on him and he will bring justice to the nations. He will not shout or cry out or raise his voice in the streets—a bruised reed, he will not break. And a smoldering wick, he will not snuff out."

In other words, He will be kind and gentle with the weak and needy. Isaiah goes to conclude, saying:

"In faithfulness he will bring forth justice. He will not falter. He will not be discouraged until he has established justice in all the earth."

God's Chosen Ones

So how do we know that God is interested in taking care of the weak and needy? Jesus tells us when He describes those in His Kingdom as His Chosen Ones. "Chosen" is the same word from the Isaiah passage. "Chosen" refers to God's electing love—that eternal love that God has put upon those in His Kingdom. "Chosen" is about being known by God. Jesus is saying that because He knows us, because He loves us, He is giving us what's best for us—just don't lose faith!

Here's the thing: even an unjust judge will relent sometimes at the persistence of a helpless widow. So how much more will the gracious, loving, choosing God hear us, and answer us with His loving kindness? It may take some time. Your prayers may not be answered immediately, or perhaps you won't receive the kind of answer that you would like.

But take heart, because God is not an unjust judge. Rather, He is a loving Judge, and His judgments towards you are based on an eternal love for those who are living in the Kingdom of God.

ADDITIONAL VERSES
FOR STUDY AND REFLECTION

1 SAMUEL 1:1-2:10

There was a certain man from Ramathaim, a Zuphite from the hill country of Ephraim, whose name was Elkanah son of Jeroham, the son of Elihu, the son of Tohu, the son of Zuph, an Ephraimite. He had two wives; one was called Hannah and the other Peninnah. Peninnah had children, but Hannah had none.

Year after year this man went up from his town to worship and sacrifice to the LORD Almighty at Shiloh, where Hophni and Phinehas, the two sons of Eli, were priests of the LORD. Whenever the day came for Elkanah to sacrifice, he would give portions of the meat to his wife Peninnah and to all her sons and daughters. But to Hannah he gave a double portion because he loved her, and the LORD had closed her womb. And because the LORD had closed her womb, her rival kept provoking her in order to irritate her. This went on year after year. Whenever Hannah went up to the house of the LORD, her rival provoked her till she wept and would not eat. Elkanah her husband would say to her, "Hannah, why are you weeping? Why don't you eat? Why are you downhearted? Don't I mean more to you than ten sons?"

Once when they had finished eating and drinking in Shiloh, Hannah stood up. Now Eli the priest was sitting on a chair by the doorpost of the LORD'S temple. In bitterness of soul Hannah wept much and prayed to the LORD. And she made a vow, saying, "O LORD Almighty, if you will only look upon your servant's misery and remember me, and not forget your servant but give her a son, then I will give him to the LORD for all the days of his life, and no razor will ever be used on his head."

As she kept on praying to the LORD, Eli observed her mouth. Hannah was praying in her heart, and her lips were moving but her voice was not heard. Eli thought she was drunk and said to her, "How long will you keep on getting drunk? Get rid of your wine."

"Not so, my lord," Hannah replied, "I am a woman who is deeply troubled. I have not been drinking wine or beer; I was pouring out my soul to the LORD. Do not take your servant for a wicked woman; I have been praying here out of my great anguish and grief."

Eli answered, "Go in peace, and may the God of Israel grant you what you have asked of him."

She said, "May your servant find favor in your eyes." Then she went her way and ate something, and her face was no longer downcast.

Early the next morning they arose and worshiped before the LORD and then went back to their home at Ramah. Elkanah lay with Hannah his wife, and the LORD remembered her. So in the course of time Hannah conceived and gave birth to a son. She named him Samuel, saying, "Because I asked the LORD for him."

When the man Elkanah went up with all his family to offer the annual sacrifice to the LORD and to fulfill his vow, Hannah did not go. She said to her husband, "After the boy is weaned, I will take him and present him before the LORD, and he will live there always."

"Do what seems best to you," Elkanah her husband told her. "Stay here until you have weaned him; only may the LORD make good his word." So the woman stayed at home and nursed her son until she had weaned him.

After he was weaned, she took the boy with her, young as he was, along with a three-year-old bull, an ephah of flour and a skin of wine, and brought him to the house of the LORD at Shiloh. When they had slaughtered the bull, they brought the boy to Eli, and she said to him, "As surely as you live, my lord, I am the woman who stood here beside you praying to the LORD. I prayed for this child, and the LORD has granted me what I asked of him. So now I give him to the LORD. For his whole life he will be given over to the LORD." And he worshiped the LORD there.

Then Hannah prayed and said:

"My heart rejoices in the LORD; in the LORD my horn is lifted high.

My mouth boasts over my enemies, for I delight in your deliverance.

"There is no one holy like the LORD; there is no one besides you; there is no Rock like our God.

"Do not keep talking so proudly or let your mouth speak such arrogance, for the LORD is a God who knows, and by him deeds are weighed.

"The bows of the warriors are broken, but those who stumbled are armed with strength.

Those who were full hire themselves out for food, but those who were hungry hunger no more.

She who was barren has borne seven children, but she who has had many sons pines away.

"The LORD brings death and makes alive; he brings down to the grave and raises up.

The LORD sends poverty and wealth; he humbles and he exalts.

He raises the poor from the dust and lifts the needy from the ash heap; he seats them with princes and has them inherit a throne of honor. "For the foundations of the earth are the LORD'S; upon them he has set the world.

He will guard the feet of his saints, but the wicked will be silenced in darkness. "It is not by strength that one prevails; those who oppose the LORD will be shattered. He will thunder against them from heaven; the LORD will judge the ends of the earth. "He will give strength to his king and exalt the horn of his anointed."

*   *   *

PSALM 102

A prayer of an afflicted man. When he is faint and pours out
his lament before the LORD.

Hear my prayer, O LORD; let my cry for help come to you. Do not hide your face from me when I am in distress.

Turn your ear to me; when I call, answer me quickly.

For my days vanish like smoke; my bones burn like glowing embers. My heart is blighted and withered like grass; I forget to eat my food. Because of my loud groaning I am reduced to skin and bones. I am like a desert owl, like an owl among the ruins. I lie awake; I have become like a bird alone on a roof. All day long my enemies taunt me; those who rail against me use my name as a curse. For I eat ashes as my food and mingle my drink with tears because of your great wrath, for you have taken me up and thrown me aside. My days are like the evening shadow; I wither away like grass.

But you, O LORD, sit enthroned forever; your renown endures through all generations. You will arise and have compassion on Zion, for it is time to show favor to her; the appointed time has come. For her stones are dear to your servants; her very dust moves them to pity. The nations will fear the name of the LORD, all the kings of the earth will revere your glory. For the LORD will rebuild Zion and appear in his glory. He will respond to the prayer of the destitute; he will not despise their plea.

Let this be written for a future generation, that a people not yet created may praise the LORD: "The LORD looked down from his sanctuary on high, from heaven he viewed the earth, to hear the groans of the prisoners and release those condemned to death." So the name of the LORD will be declared in Zion and his praise in Jerusalem when the peoples and the kingdoms assemble to worship the LORD.

In the course of my life he broke my strength; he cut short my days. So I said: "Do not take me away, O my God, in the midst of my days; your years go on through all generations. In the beginning you laid the foundations of the earth, and the heavens are the work of your hands. They will perish, but you remain; they will all wear out like a garment.

Like clothing you will change them and they will be discarded. But you remain the same, and your years will never end. The children of your servants will live in your presence; their descendants will be established before you."

*   *   *

Matthew 6:5-13

"And when you pray, do not be like the hypocrites, for they love to pray standing in the synagogues and on the street corners to be seen by men. I tell you the truth, they have received their reward in full. But when you pray, go into your room, close the door and pray to your Father, who is unseen. Then your Father, who sees what is done in secret, will reward you. And when you pray, do not keep on babbling like pagans, for they think they will be heard because of their many

words. Do not be like them, for your Father knows what you need before you ask him.

"This, then, is how you should pray: " 'Our Father in heaven, hallowed be your name,

your kingdom come, your will be done on earth as it is in heaven.

Give us today our daily bread.

Forgive us our debts, as we also have forgiven our debtors.

And lead us not into temptation, but deliver us from the evil one."

*   *   *

MARK 14:32-38

They went to a place called Gethsemane, and Jesus said to his disciples, "Sit here while I pray." He took Peter, James and John along with him, and he began to be deeply distressed and troubled. "My soul is overwhelmed with sorrow to the point of death," he said to them. "Stay here and keep watch."

Going a little farther, he fell to the ground and prayed that if possible the hour might pass from him. "Abba, Father," he said, "everything is possible for you. Take this cup from me. Yet not what I will, but what you will."

Then he returned to his disciples and found them sleeping. "Simon," he said to Peter, "are you asleep? Could you not keep watch for one hour? Watch and pray so that you will not fall into temptation. The spirit is willing, but the body is weak."

*   *   *

LUKE 11:5-13

Then he said to them, "Suppose one of you has a friend, and he goes to him at midnight and says, 'Friend, lend me three loaves of bread, because a friend of mine on a journey has come to me, and I have nothing to set before him.'

"*Then the one inside answers, 'Don't bother me. The door is already locked, and my children are with me in bed. I can't get up and give you anything.' I tell you, though he will not get up and give him the bread because he is his friend, yet because of the man's boldness he will get up and give him as much as he needs.*

"*So I say to you: Ask and it will be given to you; seek and you will find; knock and the door will be opened to you. For everyone who asks receives; he who seeks finds; and to him who knocks, the door will be opened.*

"*Which of you fathers, if your son asks for a fish, will give him a snake instead? Or if he asks for an egg, will give him a scorpion? If you then, though you are evil, know how to give good gifts to your children, how much more will your Father in heaven give the Holy Spirit to those who ask him!*"

*   *   *

1 PETER 3:12

For the eyes of the Lord are on the righteous and his ears are attentive to their prayer, but the face of the Lord is against those who do evil.

Matthew 13:1-23
Mark 4:13-20
Luke 8:11-15

The Sower

UNDERSTANDING THE PARABLE

That same day Jesus went out of the house and sat by the lake. Such large crowds gathered around him that he got into a boat and sat in it, while all the people stood on the shore. Then he told them many things in parables, saying: "A farmer went out to sow his seed. As he was scattering the seed, some fell along the path, and the birds came and ate it up. Some fell on rocky places, where it did not have much soil. It sprang up quickly, because the soil was shallow. But when the sun came up, the plants were scorched, and they withered because they had no root. Other seed fell among thorns, which grew up and choked the plants. Still other seed fell on good soil, where it produced a crop—a hundred, sixty or thirty times what was sown. He who has ears, let him hear."

The disciples came to him and asked, "Why do you speak to the people in parables?"

He replied, "The knowledge of the secrets of the kingdom of heaven has been given to you, but not to them. Whoever has will be given more, and he will have an abundance. Whoever does not have, even what he has will be taken from him. This is why I speak to them in parables: Though seeing, they do not see; though hearing, they do not hear or understand. In them is fulfilled the prophecy of Isaiah:

*'You will be ever hearing but never understanding; you will be ever
seeing but never perceiving.*

*For this people's heart has become calloused; they hardly hear with
their ears, and they have closed their eyes.*

*Otherwise they might see with their eyes, hear with their ears, under-
stand with their hearts and turn, and I would heal them.'*

*But blessed are your eyes because they see, and your ears because
they hear. For I tell you the truth, many prophets and righteous men
longed to see what you see but did not see it, and to hear what you
hear but did not hear it."* M ATT 13:1-17

           *   *   **

*"Listen then to what the parable of the sower means: When anyone
hears the message about the kingdom and does not understand it, the
evil one comes and snatches away what was sown in his heart. This
is the seed sown along the path. The one who received the seed that
fell on rocky places is the man who hears the word and at once receives it with joy. But since he has no root, he lasts only a short time.
When trouble or persecution comes because of the word, he quickly
falls away. The one who received the seed that fell among the thorns
is the man who hears the word, but the worries of this life and the
deceitfulness of wealth choke it, making it unfruitful. But the one who
received the seed that fell on good soil is the man who hears the word
and understands it. He produces a crop, yielding a hundred, sixty or
thirty times what was sown."* M ATT 13:18-23

*Then Jesus said to them, "Don't you understand this parable? How
then will you understand any parable? The farmer sows the word.
Some people are like seed along the path, where the word is sown.
As soon as they hear it, Satan comes and takes away the word that
was sown in them. Others, like seed sown on rocky places, hear the
word and at once receive it with joy. But since they have no root, they*

last only a short time. When trouble or persecution comes because of the word, they quickly fall away. Still others, like seed sown among thorns, hear the word; but the worries of this life, the deceitfulness of wealth and the desires for other things come in and choke the word, making it unfruitful. Others, like seed sown on good soil, hear the word, accept it, and produce a crop—thirty, sixty or even a hundred times what was sown. " MARK 4:13-20

"This is the meaning of the parable: The seed is the word of God. Those along the path are the ones who hear, and then the devil comes and takes away the word from their hearts, so that they may not believe and be saved. Those on the rock are the ones who receive the word with joy when they hear it, but they have no root. They believe for a while, but in the time of testing they fall away. The seed that fell among thorns stands for those who hear, but as they go on their way they are choked by life's worries, riches and pleasures, and they do not mature. But the seed on good soil stands for those with a noble and good heart, who hear the word, retain it, and by persevering produce a crop." LUKE 8:11-15

Introduction

Some things seem simple on the surface. But once you look into them you realize there is much more than you originally thought. Simplicity can be deceptive: by focusing on what you think you understand, it is possible to miss what is really there.

The parable of the Sower is like that. What can be more simple than to talk about a man going out to sow seed in different soils? It seems so obvious. Yet after Jesus told the parable to the crowd, His disciples came to Him and asked what it meant. Jesus often berated His disciples for being slow to understand, but these were not unintelligent men. Rather, as the New Testament writings of John and Peter demonstrate, many of them were quite brilliant.

The only explanation is that there is much more to the parable of the Sower than many of us realize, and that Jesus is teaching something that is not as patently obvious as we may be led to believe. The fact is, the parable of the Sower is an extraordinary piece of genius that explores the whole of Christian history from beginning to end, including the way the Kingdom of God will grow, the obstacles it will face, and the wonderful ending that will inevitably come.

Setting and Context

This parable is the first among the parables. It is one of only a handful of parables included in all three synoptic gospels (Matthew, Mark, and Luke). It is the same parable that all three gospel writers use to introduce the rest of Jesus' parables. And it is one of just a few parables that Jesus explains in detail. No other parable holds all these distinctions, and because of that, we should take special consideration not to pass it by too quickly.

Matthew tells us that when Jesus told this parable, He had been teaching by the Sea of Galilee. (It is called a sea only by tradition, since it is really just a large inland lake, about 13 miles long and 8 miles wide.) Even today it is a beautiful place. In some areas it is quiet and pastoral with grassy banks that roll down to the lake's shore. On this particular day, the crowds had swollen to such a size that Jesus got into a boat and pushed a little way off shore. The slope of the land down to the water's edge, combined with the acoustic properties of sound on water, created a natural amphitheater.

The people who sat on the shore were a mix of the local population. Some would have traveled from little villages all around to hear the new rabbi teach on God and His Kingdom. They were mostly peasants, many of them farmers. As they traveled to see Jesus, they would have had to walk down paths and roads between the countless fields that spread across the countryside.

Matthew tells us that Jesus began to teach them in parables starting with the parable of the sower. He later says that "Jesus spoke all these things to the crowd in parables; he did not say anything to them without using a parable." (Matt 13:34) We saw in the passage above that this method intrigued His disciples and they asked Him why He taught that way. His answer was rather unexpected, and it should still give us pause:

> *He replied, "The knowledge of the secrets of the kingdom of heaven has been given to you, but not to them. Whoever has will be given more, and he will have an abundance. Whoever does not have, even what he has will be taken from him. This is why I speak to them in parables: 'Though seeing, they do not see; though hearing, they do not hear or understand.'"* MATT 13:10-13

We have already discussed Jesus' practice of "veiling" His teaching with parables. As we saw in the previous chapter (Lesson 1: Hidden Treasure – Understanding the Parable), it is important to recognize that Jesus' first-century Jewish audience already had strong opinions about the Kingdom of God and the coming of the Messiah, just as Christians today hold very strong opinions about the second coming of Christ. From their interpretation of the Old Testament, everyone expected a powerful Messiah to come suddenly, wipe out the Roman oppressors, then quickly set up a magnificent, visible kingdom here on earth. Luke reveals this popular mentality when he writes: "[Jesus] went on to tell them a parable, because he was near Jerusalem and the people thought that the kingdom of God was going to appear at once." (Luke 19:11)

The problem with this popular interpretation was that it was wrong. In complete disregard of everyone's assumptions and expectations, God sent a suffering servant to establish a spiritual kingdom that would slowly grow to fill "the entire earth" (Dan 2:35). This true Kingdom would certainly have physical manifestations – but not those assumed by Jesus' audience.

That was the secret. *Unless listeners understood that the parables were all about Jesus and His unique ministry, they could not understand the parables.*[1] The secret that had been revealed to the disciples was Jesus Himself and His unexpected method of redemption. The people who came to hear Jesus this particular day were expecting a conquering king who would set up His Messianic kingdom in great splendor from Jerusalem. Instead, Jesus told them that the Kingdom would spread like seed from the hand of a sower. That's a radical difference.

But how is it that this knowledge had been given to the disciples and not to the people? Jesus explains this later in an exchange with Peter. "Who do people say that I am?" Jesus asked. The people had many wrong answers: He was John the Baptist come back to life, or Elijah, or some other prophet. Peter, however, said: "You are the Christ [Messiah], the Son of the Living God." Jesus' response explains the true source of Simon Peter's wisdom: "Blessed are you, Simon son of Jonah, for this was not revealed to you by man, but by my Father in heaven." (Matt 16:17)

In other words, God Himself had personally revealed the truth about who Jesus was to the disciples. It was a spiritual revelation via a direct action of God. The rationale behind it was that these same disciples were eventually going to take this mysterious message Jesus had taught in parables and explain it clearly to the people. This would happen *after* Jesus' death and resurrection. We see it happening in Acts. The death and resurrection of Jesus was the great key unlocking the general teaching of the parables, but it was too much for the people to understand right then.[2] In fact, it was too much for anyone to understand; just look how often the disciples misunderstood Jesus!

But we shouldn't be too hard on them. The Holy Spirit,

whose role is to guide people into the truth, had not yet
begun to indwell believers like He did after Jesus' resurrection. (John 16:13) The only reason Jesus' first coming
seems clearer to us now is *because* God's plan worked out as He
intended. Furthermore, the Holy Spirit has been poured
out across the earth ensuring that countless people will
understand Jesus for who He truly is: the Son of God. But
at the time Jesus was telling the parables to the people, these
things were not at all clear.

Jesus anticipated this, of course. In Luke's version, after
Jesus finished explaining the parable of the sower to His
disciples, He told them a few more things to consider: "No
one lights a lamp and hides it in a jar or puts it under a bed.
Instead, he puts it on a stand, so that those who come in
can see the light. For there is nothing hidden that will not
be disclosed, and nothing concealed that will not be known
or brought out into the open. Therefore consider carefully
how you listen. Whoever has will be given more; whoever does
not have, even what he thinks he has will be taken from him."
(Luke 8:16-18)

When He said this, Jesus was referring to the upcoming
world-wide proclamation about Him after His resurrection:
the lamp is the message of the gospel; it will not be hidden
anymore but will be put on a stand for all the world to see
its light. In other words, the teaching that is hidden in the
parables will be brought out into the open. Those who have
been given this teaching by God will be given salvation and
much more; those who have not been given this teaching, who
do not understand who Jesus is, will have what they think they
have (which is really nothing) taken away in the Judgment.[3]

This context is very important to recognize when looking at
the parable of the sower. At its heart, it is about how the message
of the Kingdom goes out and how people respond to it. Jesus'
quotation from Isaiah 6 is not immediately encouraging:

You will be ever hearing but never understanding; you will be ever seeing but never perceiving. For this people's heart has become calloused; they hardly hear with their ears, and they have closed their eyes. Otherwise they might see with their eyes, hear with their ears, understand with their hearts and turn, and I would heal them.

The quotation comes from Isaiah's commissioning as a prophet: God will judge the people for their hardened hearts and closed ears. For hundreds of years the people had rejected God and His law, so the time of judgment had come. Isaiah, however, was a prophet of both judgment and hope. Immediately after God said in chapter 6 that He would judge the people by wiping out their cities, He follows it by graciously predicting (in the next chapter) that a "holy seed" would grow into a new tree, and that "a virgin shall be with child".

What was Jesus communicating when He quoted these verses? Those who will not submit to His message will be judged, and His manner of presenting the message (in parables) will enforce that judgment. Is it not interesting, therefore, that the parable concerns itself with four types of hearers?

Jesus went on to explain the specific parallels between the soils and the hearers. Mark tells us that right before He explained the parable, He criticized the disciples for their lack of comprehension: if they didn't understand that parable, "how then will you understand any parable?" (Mark 4:13) In other words, "listen up, because I'm going to explain how parables work."

The parable is clearly allegorical. That is, specific elements in the story symbolize specific things Jesus is trying to teach. The natural world (a sower, seed, soil) is being compared to the spiritual world (Jesus, word of God, hearers). There is a clear tit-for-tat comparison. As we have seen previously, not all of Jesus' parables have this clear a comparison between two specific things. The fact that this one does shows us that Jesus did not want us to miss anything.

So what exactly is the parable talking about?

The Sower

A farmer went out to sow his seed. MATT 13:3

JESUS' INTERPRETATION:
Listen then to what the parable of the sower means: When anyone hears the message about the kingdom... MATT 13:18-19
The farmer sows the word. MARK 4:14
This is the meaning of the parable: The seed is the word of God. LUKE 8:11

First-century Israel was an agricultural community. A large majority of the population was directly involved in farming, and those who were not were immersed in the agricultural society. The Jewish religious calendar included seven great feasts, two of which reflected God's blessings on the harvest cycle (the Feasts of Firstfruits and Weeks). Just as everyone today is familiar with a grocery store, everyone then was familiar with the wheat farmer: he provided people with their daily bread.

In the film *The Sower,* Mr. Dement points out that wheat is a winter annual. In the Northern Hemisphere, it is sown in early Autumn, left to develop slowly through the Winter, then in the Spring grows quickly until the harvest in early Summer. The farmer in the parable would have followed this same growing schedule. During his planting he would have used a canvas bag slung over his shoulder and filled with wheat seed from the prior year's harvest.[4] He would then have spread the seed by hand as he walked from one side of his field to the other. It is a picture that Jesus' audience would have seen countless times.

It is a simple picture. Yet it is this simplicity of the parable *in light of what Jesus is comparing it to* that makes it so intriguing and unexpected. In contradiction of every contemporary expectation, Jesus is saying that the new world-transforming force of His Messianic kingdom will move through the earth just like a sower spreads his seed — and nothing more dramatically than that.[5]

It mystified Jesus' audience. Wasn't the Messiah supposed to be a conquering king who, like Alexander the Great, would roll back his enemies with effortless ease? According to this parable, no: the Messiah will spread His Kingdom like a man sowing his seed. To be more specific, Jesus — the one spreading the message of the Kingdom — is comparing Himself to an ordinary farmer; and His message of the Kingdom is like seed falling on soil. Instead of battles and trumpets, Jesus is saying that the word of God is the most important thing in the Kingdom's spread.

But what a radical claim! Standing two thousand years after Christ's inauguration of His Kingdom, we enjoy much of the fruit of the success of His word as it has spread through the nations. Yet even today many people overlook the fact that it is the word of God that is the dynamic force behind the spread of the Kingdom of God. Not church events, not programs, not exciting music - it is the message of the Kingdom that matters.

That said, what does this parable teach us about the word of God and the one who spreads it?

First, the Kingdom is actively being planted and grown for the harvest. Jesus is personally pushing along its growth through His disciples who act as local sowers wherever they may be. He started this with His earthly ministry and continues it from heaven to this day. His goal is to spread His Kingdom across the entire earth.

Second, the seed has within it the potential to grow an entire harvest out of just one seed. There is enormous genetic complexity within a seed: by simply putting it in the soil and adding the right elements, it naturally grows into a new plant, multiplying itself enormously. Think of Mr. Dement holding up the wheat plant with twelve tillers coming out of one seed. Each tiller will bear heads of wheat, and those heads have within them the potential to grow more and more wheat, all following the law of exponential return.

The word of God found in the Bible has the same compact potential. Christ has grown His entire Church from this single book that carries His message of the Kingdom in it. Everything necessary for limitless growth is found within those pages. And as the history of the church clearly demonstrates, it has grown from Jerusalem, to Samaria, to the ends of the earth. (Acts 1:8).

Third, the seed and the soil were made for each other. There is a perfect balance and unity in their relationship. So too, the word of God and man were made for each other. The primary purpose of the word of God is to create new life in the hearts of men, women and children everywhere. It was designed to change people dramatically, to take the elements of their personalities and bear more fruit for the Kingdom.

Fourth, there is an important sense of time passing in the parable. Most of us living in the modern world have little contact with agricultural society. As a result, it is easy to overlook this aspect of the story. But time plays a key role in the world of the farmer since plants do not grow in a day. Rather, many months pass from the time the seed goes into the ground to the time of the harvest.

This passage of time in the parable provides an important commentary on the chronology of the Kingdom. Just as the sowing marks the commencement of the crop, so too does Jesus' preaching mark the commencement of the Kingdom. In the same way, the harvest marks the end of the season just as the final Judgment will mark the end of the age and the consummation of the eternal Kingdom. The sequence of events in the parable is a wonderful picture of the present and future aspects of the Kingdom. It began at a specific time, continues through the present, and will be consummated in the future at the harvest.

After all, the ultimate goal of planting the seed is the great and fruitful harvest. This is the only reason the seed is being planted: to grow up and bear a crop for the farmer. There are really only two ends the parable entertains: being fruitless

or fruitful. And although there are some instances of the former, the latter is assured in great measure.

Along the Path

> *As he was scattering the seed, some fell along the path, and the birds*
> *came and ate it up.* MATT 13:4

> JESUS' INTERPRETATION:
> *When anyone hears the message about the kingdom and does not un-*
> *derstand it, the evil one comes and snatches away what was sown in*
> *his heart. This is the seed sown along the path.* MATT 13:19
> *Some people are like seed along the path, where the word is sown. As*
> *soon as they hear it, Satan comes and takes away the word that was*
> *sown in them.* MARK 4:15
> *Those along the path are the ones who hear, and then the devil comes*
> *and takes away the word from their hearts, so that they may not be-*
> *lieve and be saved.* LUKE 8:12

As Mr. Dement explained in the film, it is natural to have
seed fall on the roadways bordering fields. Such an overflow
is a consequence of seeding by hand. In the first century,
the land was divided up into arable portions with paths running between them for access or for travelers. It is a simple
picture to imagine the seeds falling on the hard-packed
ground, then being trampled by feet (as Luke tells us) and
eventually eaten by birds.

The first comparison is between the hard path and those
who reject the word of God immediately. Jesus' own ministry
was filled with people who were hard paths. Just a few chapters
before, Matthew recounts how Jesus proclaimed woes on a
number of the cities who did not repent even though they had
seen many of Jesus' miracles. (Matt 11:20-24)

The second comparison is between the birds and Satan.

Jesus tells us that as soon as some hear, Satan comes and takes away the word. Exactly how he does this is not said, but clearly he has spiritual influence over those who are his. This actually explains a lot about those people who reject Christianity out-of-hand, almost without thinking about it. Some of us today don't like to consider the spiritual powers that surround us, and although they certainly can be taken out of context, in instances where people are blatantly rejecting the word, Jesus tells us that Satan has a direct hand in this rejection. As we learn from the Apostle John, Satan "leads the whole world astray." (Rev 12:9)

This should remind us that there are two kingdoms at war in the world. The kingdom of Satan strives against the Kingdom of God, and there are gains and losses on both sides. We know from the Bible that Christ's Kingdom is already victorious — but it does not mean that Satan and his minions have given up the fight. Satan wants as many hearts and minds as he can have before the end.

Matthew gives us additional insight into what happens in the heart of this type of hearer: he does not *understand* the word of God. A spiritual comprehension of the things of God is necessary to accept them. Isaiah prophesied this lack of understanding in the passage Jesus quoted between His telling and explanation of the parable. The verb "to understand" can also be translated "to grasp" or "to comprehend" and refers to taking Jesus' teaching to heart, to living it, as opposed to merely listening and not letting it go any deeper.[6]

The Rocky Soil

Some fell on rocky places, where it did not have much soil. It sprang up quickly, because the soil was shallow. But when the sun came up, the plants were scorched, and they withered because they had no root.
MATT 13:5

JESUS' INTERPRETATION:

The one who received the seed that fell on rocky places is the man who hears the word and at once receives it with joy. But since he has no root, he lasts only a short time. When trouble or persecution comes because of the word, he quickly falls away. MATT 13:20-21

Others, like seed sown on rocky places, hear the word and at once receive it with joy. But since they have no root, they last only a short time. When trouble or persecution comes because of the word, they quickly fall away. MARK 4:16-17

Those on the rock are the ones who receive the word with joy when they hear it, but they have no root. They believe for a while, but in the time of testing they fall away. LUKE 8:13

In many of the fields near where Jesus preached were large slabs of limestone lying just beneath the surface of the soil. During the summer months, the limestone soaked up the heat of the sun and retained it. In early Autumn, the sower planted his seed, then the rains came to water the soil. As the temperature dropped, the layers of rock beneath the ground would continue to release heat into the soil causing the seeds above them to grow quickly due to the presence of warmth and moisture, faster even than the seed in the better soil surrounding them.[7]

But it was a deceptive growth. After the Winter thaw, the Spring came and the heat of early Summer. Because of the rocky substratum, the wheat plants couldn't grow the roots necessary to soak up water and nutrients for long-term growth. As the days grew hotter, the plants in shallow soil would eventually die.

This second type of soil represents those in the church with shallow belief. Their quick growth corresponds to the initial joy and excitement of some new believers. This does not mean that all early joy is superficial, but rather that some excitement masks the lack of true growth in some new believers and will reveal itself with time.

The rocks correspond to the things inside their hearts that keep them from growing roots and deepening in their faith. This has nothing to do with good intentions, for some people mean well when they come into the church. They have seen the fruit borne by true believers and have sensed their own need for Jesus Christ.

But deep inside they will not accept parts of the gospel. There is a lack of genuine submission to God and His word in their lives. As a result, when the world tests their level of commitment to God, they are found wanting. This testing can come through social pressures from family members, friends, co-workers or spouses. It often requires making decisions for the Kingdom that are uncomfortable or even painful. In these cases, the young plants wither and die under the heat of persecution.

The Weeds

Other seed fell among thorns, which grew up and choked the plants.
MATT 13:7

JESUS' INTERPRETATION:
The one who received the seed that fell among the thorns is the man who hears the word, but the worries of this life and the deceitfulness of wealth choke it, making it unfruitful. MATT 13:22
Still others, like seed sown among thorns, hear the word; but the worries of this life, the deceitfulness of wealth and the desires for other things come in and choke the word, making it unfruitful. MARK 4:18
The seed that fell among thorns stands for those who hear, but as they go on their way they are choked by life's worries, riches and pleasures, and they do not mature. LUKE 8:14

In the film *The Sower*, Mr. Dement explains how "competition" from the weeds can choke out the good plants. This is an excellent perspective on the third type of soil. It is fertile, it has plenty of moisture and depth, and it allows the plants to take root. Yet it is not what the soil *lacks* but what it has *in addition to* the seed that is the problem.[8]

The issue is that the weeds compete for the nutrients and light, and essentially take away the strength of the growing wheat plant. Furthermore, weeds often grow much faster than the wheat. If steps are not taken against them, they will swarm up over a crop and choke it out.

As Jesus explained, the weeds correspond to the worries of life, the deception of riches and pleasures, and the desires for things other than God. All these work together to keep a healthy plant from bearing fruit. It is as if the plant does everything *but* the one thing it is supposed to do. Instead, it slowly stops growing and becomes ineffective.

Of the three types of soils, this type is the one that has the most parallels in the modern Christian church. What are the worries of this life? Anything that causes us to lose focus on God's provision for us, whether it is our work, our family, or our own lives. All of these things are good when looked at in light of the Kingdom of God, but on their own, outside of God's word, they become a source of worry. Such concern is a debilitating factor, something that mortgages today on behalf of an uncontrollable tomorrow. As Jesus told His disciples, "Therefore I tell you, do not worry about your life, what you will eat; or about your body, what you will wear. Life is more than food, and the body more than clothes." (Luke 12:22-23)

Jesus next labels riches, wealth, and pleasures as factors that will choke out the life of a believer. Although it would be convenient to say that only those at the highest income bracket fall in this category, Americans as a whole are some of the wealthiest Christians in the world. Other nationalities can quickly see how Americans are plagued by their riches. Again, it comes down to competition: do financial means occupy one's focus more than bearing fruit for the Kingdom? *How much* you have isn't really the issue so much as whether or not you treat financial or material concerns as more important than the Kingdom of God. If you do, you won't bear fruit.

The Good Soil

Still other seed fell on good soil, where it produced a crop—a hundred, sixty or thirty times what was sown. MATT 13:8

JESUS' INTERPRETATION:
But the one who received the seed that fell on good soil is the man who hears the word and understands it. He produces a crop, yielding a hundred, sixty or thirty times what was sown. MATT 13:23
Others, like seed sown on good soil, hear the word, accept it, and produce a crop—thirty, sixty or even a hundred times what was sown. MARK 4:20
But the seed on good soil stands for those with a noble and good heart, who hear the word, retain it, and by persevering produce a crop. LUKE 8:15

As we arrive at the fourth type of soil, we come to the purpose of the sower's work: to produce a bountiful crop. Jesus gives us specific figures for returns on what was sown. As Mr. Dement explained, this refers to the amount of grain harvested based on how much was sown. In modern times, a 40-60x increase is excellent. Jesus says that the spiritual harvest could be even greater than that at 100x the return.

How is this possible? Again, as Mr. Dement showed in the field, one seed of wheat will grow into a crown that has multiple tillers growing out of it (in the case of the film, a dozen tillers were growing from one crown). Each tiller has the potential to produce a head of wheat, which in turn can have 10 or more grains of wheat in it. Obviously, not all seeds produce this many tillers (especially if they are planted close together), and not all tillers produce heads of wheat. Some produce more than others, as Jesus' numbers seem to indicate. When all are taken together, however, there is a marvelous and miraculous crop.

Although we don't see the harvest in this parable, it is clearly implied since one has to harvest the crop to know how much it has provided. Again, the harvest is where everything is headed: it is the point of bearing fruit.

The comparisons continue at this simple level. In this case, the good soil is compared to those with a noble and good heart — in other words, those who understand the word, who take it inside and retain it, and who persevere in their faith. All these attributes are found in the hearers who are like good soil; they are true disciples of Jesus. As Jesus told His disciples, "This is to my Father's glory, that you bear much fruit, showing yourselves to be my disciples." (John 15:8)

And what is that fruit? It stems from a heart transformed by the Holy Spirit. Jesus explained in the Sermon on the Mount that the true fruit is being poor in spirit, sorry for one's sins, meek toward others, hungry for righteousness, merciful, pure in heart, and a peacemaker. These are the things that matter to God. Furthermore, such fruit is how Jesus spreads His Kingdom: as St. Francis of Assisi said, "Preach the gospel at all times, and when necessary use words."

Having Ears to Hear

He who has ears, let him hear. MATT 13:9

The use of ears as a symbol for hearing has a long precedent in the Old Testament. Jesus was not the first to use this phrase: all of the great prophets used variations on it; it is found in the Wisdom books; and it goes all the way back to Deuteronomy, when Moses tells the people, "with your own eyes you saw those great trials, those miraculous signs and great wonders.

But to this day the LORD has not given you a mind that understands or eyes that see or ears that hear." (Deut 29:3-4)

The idea behind the symbol is fairly straightforward: those who listen and obey God from their hearts have ears to hear; those who do not have either "stopped up" their ears or simply don't have ears with which to listen to God. This is an example of using the natural world to reflect something spiritual. It is the people's responsibility to recognize that He is the Messiah. Their own unrealistic expectations and sinful rejections are all signs that they cannot hear what He is saying.

There are, however, those who can hear Him. The disciples have been given ears to hear. And there are many others in the New Testament who listen to what Jesus is saying *and change their lives as a result.*

Hearing is not about registering the words but about taking them in, truly understanding and bearing fruit. If a person does not bear fruit as a result, that person does not have ears to hear. Sadly, there are some in the church today who listen to many true things, but by virtue of being hard ground, or rocky soil, or covered in weeds, they do not have ears to hear.

Summary

In closing, we see in this parable the history of the world from the start of Jesus' ministry to the end of time. The Kingdom will advance not by swords and outward battles, but by the simple preaching of the word of God. There will inevitably be some losses (and disciples should expect this), but those losses pale in comparison to the great and wonderful harvest that will ultimately result. The four types of soil describe all the potential hearers of the gospel message. But only those who hear, and act on what they hear by bearing fruit, are truly part of the Kingdom.

PARALLELS

ORIGINAL PARABLE	PARABLE FILM
The sower.	Jesus or one of His disciples.
Sowing the seed.	Preaching the message of the Kingdom.
The seed.	The Word of God or the message of the Kingdom.
The path.	Those who do not accept the Word at all.
Birds flying down and eating up the seed.	Satan coming and taking away the Word that was sown in them.
The rocky soil.	Those who hear the Word and receive it with joy. But since they have no root, they last only a short time.
The heat of the sun.	Trouble or persecution.
The weed-infested soil.	Those who hear the Word, but the worries of this life and the deceitfulness of wealth choke it, making it unfruitful.
The weeds.	The worries of this life, deceitfulness of wealth, and desire for other things.
The good soil.	Those who hear the Word and understand it because they have a noble and good heart. They produce a crop, yielding a hundred, sixty or thirty times what was sown.
The crop.	The good works of the Kingdom.

Endnotes

1 Herman Ridderbos, *The Coming of the Kingdom* (P&R, 1962), 123.

2 Ridderbos, 135.

3 Ridderbos, 134-135.

4 Simon J. Kistemaker, *The Parables* (Baker, 2006), 32.

5 Ridderbos, 132.

6 Arland Hultgren, *The Parables of Jesus* (Eerdmans, 2002), 195.

7 Kistemaker, 38.

8 Kistemaker, 39.

Matthew 13:1-23
Mark 4:13-20
Luke 8:11-15

The Sower

LIVING THE PARABLE

That same day Jesus went out of the house and sat by the lake. Such large crowds gathered around him that he got into a boat and sat in it, while all the people stood on the shore. Then he told them many things in parables, saying: "A farmer went out to sow his seed. As he was scattering the seed, some fell along the path, and the birds came and ate it up. Some fell on rocky places, where it did not have much soil. It sprang up quickly, because the soil was shallow. But when the sun came up, the plants were scorched, and they withered because they had no root. Other seed fell among thorns, which grew up and choked the plants. Still other seed fell on good soil, where it produced a crop—a hundred, sixty or thirty times what was sown. He who has ears, let him hear."

The disciples came to him and asked, "Why do you speak to the people in parables?"

He replied, "The knowledge of the secrets of the kingdom of heaven has been given to you, but not to them. Whoever has will be given more, and he will have an abundance. Whoever does not have, even what he has will be taken from him. This is why I speak to them in parables: Though seeing, they do not see; though hearing, they do not hear or understand. In them is fulfilled the prophecy of Isaiah:

'You will be ever hearing but never understanding; you will be ever
seeing but never perceiving.

For this people's heart has become calloused; they hardly hear with
their ears, and they have closed their eyes.

Otherwise they might see with their eyes, hear with their ears, understand with their hearts and turn, and I would heal them.'

But blessed are your eyes because they see, and your ears because
they hear. For I tell you the truth, many prophets and righteous men
longed to see what you see but did not see it, and to hear what you
hear but did not hear it." MATT 13:1-17

*   *   *

"Listen then to what the parable of the sower means: When anyone
hears the message about the kingdom and does not understand it, the
evil one comes and snatches away what was sown in his heart. This
is the seed sown along the path. The one who received the seed that
fell on rocky places is the man who hears the word and at once receives it with joy. But since he has no root, he lasts only a short time.
When trouble or persecution comes because of the word, he quickly
falls away. The one who received the seed that fell among the thorns
is the man who hears the word, but the worries of this life and the
deceitfulness of wealth choke it, making it unfruitful. But the one who
received the seed that fell on good soil is the man who hears the word
and understands it. He produces a crop, yielding a hundred, sixty or
thirty times what was sown." MATT 13:18-23

Then Jesus said to them, "Don't you understand this parable? How
then will you understand any parable? The farmer sows the word.
Some people are like seed along the path, where the word is sown.
As soon as they hear it, Satan comes and takes away the word that
was sown in them. Others, like seed sown on rocky places, hear the
word and at once receive it with joy. But since they have no root, they

last only a short time. When trouble or persecution comes because of the word, they quickly fall away. Still others, like seed sown among thorns, hear the word; but the worries of this life, the deceitfulness of wealth and the desires for other things come in and choke the word, making it unfruitful. Others, like seed sown on good soil, hear the word, accept it, and produce a crop—thirty, sixty or even a hundred times what was sown." MARK 4:13-20

"This is the meaning of the parable: The seed is the word of God. Those along the path are the ones who hear, and then the devil comes and takes away the word from their hearts, so that they may not believe and be saved. Those on the rock are the ones who receive the word with joy when they hear it, but they have no root. They believe for a while, but in the time of testing they fall away. The seed that fell among thorns stands for those who hear, but as they go on their way they are choked by life's worries, riches and pleasures, and they do not mature. But the seed on good soil stands for those with a noble and good heart, who hear the word, retain it, and by persevering produce a crop." LUKE 8:11-15

TRANSCRIPT OF APPLICATION VIDEO

Living out The Sower – Dr. Frank Lewis

Dr. Frank Lewis is Senior Pastor of First Baptist Church in Nashville, Tennessee.

Introduction

The first time I saw the film *The Sower*, I was amazed at how much Mr. Dement knew about wheat. He knows not only how to plant it, but he knows how to nurture it. He knows how it grows, he knows how to watch for every stage of its development. And he's real excited about the harvest when that time comes.

I got to thinking about it, and even though I'm not a farmer, Mr. Dement and I have a lot in common. As a pastor,

God has called me to work in His field. I sow seed everywhere I go. Sometimes it's through the pulpit. Sometimes it's in the daily interactions I have with people downtown or in the office, or in the hospital. Lots of places where I go, I always find myself broadcasting that seed as I take my steps around.

Seeing Ourselves as Soil

You see, when Jesus paints this picture of our hearts being like soil, it is an accurate picture of the way every one of us finds ourselves. When we think of our hearts being hard, or stony, or weed-infested, or good soil, the important thing for us to consider in this parable is, "What kind of soil am I?"

First of all, there are limitations to comparing the human heart to soil. Soil doesn't really change that much. But because of the powerful work of the Holy Spirit, the heart can change—it can radically change. I think that's one of the reasons why Jesus uses this portrayal of the Sower. It's such an accurate depiction of what happens when the seed of the Gospel is sown. Jesus uses this as both a warning as well as an instruction. Our hearts are either going to be the hardened soil, the rocky soil, the weed-infested soil, our hearts may be good soil. What kind of soil are you?

The Hard Path

When Jesus tells this parable, He makes the point that Satan comes in to the hard heart and removes the seed before the seed ever has the opportunity to put down its roots and grow. Sometimes as we're sharing the Gospel and doing those acts of kindness to minister to people, we will find or sense that they are rejecting us. They're mad, they're angry, they hold the message of God with great contempt in their life—they don't want to hear it. They'll even tell us so. Sometimes our tendency might be to feel like they're rejecting us, but the truth is, they're rejecting our message.

When that happens, it's very important for us, if we're going to be faithful to the task of sowing seeds, to do a couple of things. One, we should try to be very sensitive to their response and not treat them in the same way. Their anger and frustration with the message is not the same thing we need to give back to them. Instead, we should follow Jesus' example and pray for these people. We should remember that Satan is at work in their lives and their hearts are hard, and the Holy Spirit may not have begun His work of softening their hearts to respond to the Gospel. By praying for them, there is no telling how their hearts are going to be moved and what forces God may use to bring change to the soil of their lives.

The Rocky Soil

The next soil we come to is the rocky soil. It may not look like it, but as Mr. Dement said, the rocks are beneath the surface. When seed gets scattered on soil like this, it may spring up quickly, but the roots go down and encounter resistance. When that happens, there's no chance for them to grow: they sprang up quickly, but there was no opportunity for them to produce fruit.

As a new Christian comes to this new experience of faith, it seems like there are times when the joy and the enthusiasm of the Christian life springs up quickly, but then suddenly they find themselves without that joy. One of the reasons that happens is because of rejection—their friends, their family, the people that were closest to them before they came to know Christ have suddenly rejected them because of this newfound faith.

It also happens when we encounter times of testing and trial. Maybe a crisis comes into a person's life and shakes their faith. Some of the best things that you can do today are to surround yourself with some of the Christian disciplines that will help in times like these.

Pastorally, I want to guarantee something to every one of you, especially those of you who are new Christians. You are going to experience times of testing and trial. You're going to go through a crisis sooner or later, and when that happens the disciplines you've incorporated in your life are going to keep you from withering like these plants.

First, make a commitment to read the scriptures daily. Read the Bible. Find out what it is that God's Word has to say to you. In God's Word is life, you'll grow, you'll discover more about this wonderful gift of salvation that is yours. Spend some time everyday in prayer. Prayer is simply communication with your Father. As His child, He wants to hear from you. Just spending time with your Heavenly Father—what a joy that is. Then there's also fellowship with other believers. If you're new to your faith, look for someone in your church or small group whose spiritual maturity is an encouragement to you. Find someone who has already been there and done that. Find someone who has gone through some trials, who has endured some tough times. And you'll find great encouragement in getting to know them and learning their stories. Even ask them if it's possible to maybe spend one day a week just talking to them about what it really means to be a believer or learning how to pray.

Jesus wants us to grow. He wants us to produce a full harvest. The best way for this to happen in our lives is to put Bible study, prayer, and fellowship with believers as the top priorities.

The Weed-Infested Soil

The third kind of soil in the parable is soil that's become infested with weeds. As you can see, we're standing right at the edge of Mr. Dement's field where he has planted some crops, but the weeds here are so strong they've taken over. There's no way other plants can grow because these weeds are stealing all the nutrition.

When Jesus tells this parable to the people who are His first audience, as well as when we hear it in our day and time, it's not hard to miss the application. We hear the good news of the Gospel, it's life changing, our hearts resonate with it, but if we're not careful the concerns of this world will just take over everything.

In American Christianity, it seems that we are even guilty of this addiction to technology, an addiction to materialism. We want more, bigger, better, faster. It seems we always have to take something to the next level because what we have is just not good enough. Jesus knows that about us.

In addition to that, some doctors even have diagnosed some people with what they call "hurry sickness." Hurry sickness is when there's so much on your schedule there's not time in your day to write one more appointment. You're so anxious about getting to the next place, you're flying through life without ever stopping to realize that you're living. Jesus knows that this tendency to be consumed by other things will kill off the potential of the Gospel to take its root and develop fruit—bearing Christians. Remember, you cannot bear the kind of fruit Jesus wants if weeds have snuffed out all the vitality, which leaves us wilting and dying. Jesus wants us to be fruitful.

The Good Soil

We finally come to the seed that's fallen on good soil—and that one tiny seed produces a crop much, much, much, greater than itself. I think the final thing that we need to remember about this parable is to ask ourselves the question "what kind of soil are we?" We're either hard soil, we're soil with rocks just beneath the surface, we're soil with weeds crowding out the good things of the gospel, or like good soil, the Holy Spirit takes the Word of God, applies it to our hearts and we become part of this harvest that's vast beyond measure.

I'm reminded of a couple things as I reconsider this

parable today. One is that there are people all around me who are at any one of these stages. Some are hardened to the Gospel. Some are so enamored by material things that they can't even listen to the ideas of the Kingdom of God right now. And yet I have the privilege of sowing the seed, thus bringing forth the harvest that He chooses. The other thing that I have to remind myself is that my heart must always be soft to hear the whisper of God.

Today, wherever you are, whoever you are, as you study this parable, I hope you'll remember that you have a part in God's Kingdom.

ADDITIONAL VERSES
FOR STUDY AND REFLECTION

Luke 4:14-30

Jesus returned to Galilee in the power of the Spirit, and news about him spread through the whole countryside. He taught in their synagogues, and everyone praised him.

He went to Nazareth, where he had been brought up, and on the Sabbath day he went into the synagogue, as was his custom. And he stood up to read. The scroll of the prophet Isaiah was handed to him. Unrolling it, he found the place where it is written:

"The Spirit of the Lord is on me, because he has anointed me to preach good news to the poor.

He has sent me to proclaim freedom for the prisoners and recovery of sight for the blind, to release the oppressed, to proclaim the year of the Lord's favor."

Then he rolled up the scroll, gave it back to the attendant and sat down. The eyes of everyone in the synagogue were fastened on him, and he began by saying to them, "Today this scripture is fulfilled in your hearing."

All spoke well of him and were amazed at the gracious words that came from his lips. "Isn't this Joseph's son?" they asked.

Jesus said to them, "Surely you will quote this proverb to me: 'Physician, heal yourself! Do here in your hometown what we have heard that you did in Capernaum.'"

"I tell you the truth," he continued, "no prophet is accepted in his hometown. I assure you that there were many widows in Israel in Elijah's time, when the sky was shut for three and a half years and there was a severe famine throughout the land. Yet Elijah was not sent to any of them, but to a widow in Zarephath in the region of Sidon. And there were many in Israel with leprosy in the time of Elisha the prophet, yet not one of them was cleansed—only Naaman the Syrian."

All the people in the synagogue were furious when they heard this. They got up, drove him out of the town, and took him to the brow of the hill on which the town was built, in order to throw him down the cliff. But he walked right through the crowd and went on his way.

*   *   *

ACTS 2:14; 40-41

Then Peter stood up with the Eleven, raised his voice and addressed the crowd: "Fellow Jews and all of you who live in Jerusalem, let me explain this to you; listen carefully to what I say....With many other words he warned them; and he pleaded with them, "Save yourselves from this corrupt generation." Those who accepted his message were baptized, and about three thousand were added to their number that day.

*   *   *

ACTS 17:32-34

When they heard about the resurrection of the dead, some of them sneered, but others said, "We want to hear you again on this subject."

At that, Paul left the Council. A few men became followers of Paul and believed. Among them was Dionysius, a member of the Areopagus, also a woman named Damaris, and a number of others.

1 JOHN 2:19

They went out from us, but they did not really belong to us. For if they had belonged to us, they would have remained with us; but their going showed that none of them belonged to us.

*   *   *

JOHN 6:60-69

On hearing it, many of his disciples said, "This is a hard teaching. Who can accept it?"

Aware that his disciples were grumbling about this, Jesus said to them, "Does this offend you? What if you see the Son of Man ascend to where he was before! The Spirit gives life; the flesh counts for nothing. The words I have spoken to you are spirit and they are life. Yet there are some of you who do not believe." For Jesus had known from the beginning which of them did not believe and who would betray him. He went on to say, "This is why I told you that no one can come to me unless the Father has enabled him."

From this time many of his disciples turned back and no longer followed him.

"You do not want to leave too, do you?" Jesus asked the Twelve.

Simon Peter answered him, "Lord, to whom shall we go? You have the words of eternal life. We believe and know that you are the Holy One of God."

1 TIMOTHY 6:9-11

*People who want to get rich fall into temptation and a trap and into
many foolish and harmful desires that plunge men into ruin and destruction. For the love of money is a root of all kinds of evil. Some
people, eager for money, have wandered from the faith and pierced
themselves with many griefs.*

*But you, man of God, flee from all this, and pursue righteousness,
godliness, faith, love, endurance and gentleness.*

*   *   *

LUKE 12:16-31

*And he told them this parable: "The ground of a certain rich man
produced a good crop. He thought to himself, 'What shall I do? I
have no place to store my crops.'*

*"Then he said, 'This is what I'll do. I will tear down my barns and
build bigger ones, and there I will store all my grain and my goods.
And I'll say to myself, "You have plenty of good things laid up for
many years. Take life easy; eat, drink and be merry."'*

*"But God said to him, 'You fool! This very night your life will be
demanded from you. Then who will get what you have prepared for
yourself?'*

*"This is how it will be with anyone who stores up things for himself
but is not rich toward God."*

*Then Jesus said to his disciples: "Therefore I tell you, do not worry
about your life, what you will eat; or about your body, what you will
wear. Life is more than food, and the body more than clothes. Consider
the ravens: They do not sow or reap, they have no storeroom or barn;
yet God feeds them. And how much more valuable you are than birds!
Who of you by worrying can add a single hour to his life? Since you
cannot do this very little thing, why do you worry about the rest?*

"Consider how the lilies grow. They do not labor or spin. Yet I

tell you, not even Solomon in all his splendor was dressed like one of these. If that is how God clothes the grass of the field, which is here today, and tomorrow is thrown into the fire, how much more will he clothe you, O you of little faith! And do not set your heart on what you will eat or drink; do not worry about it. For the pagan world runs after all such things, and your Father knows that you need them. But seek his kingdom, and these things will be given to you as well.

*   *   *

John 15:1-16

"I am the true vine, and my Father is the gardener. He cuts off every branch in me that bears no fruit, while every branch that does bear fruit he prunes so that it will be even more fruitful. You are already clean because of the word I have spoken to you. Remain in me, and I will remain in you. No branch can bear fruit by itself; it must remain in the vine. Neither can you bear fruit unless you remain in me.

"I am the vine; you are the branches. If a man remains in me and I in him, he will bear much fruit; apart from me you can do nothing. If anyone does not remain in me, he is like a branch that is thrown away and withers; such branches are picked up, thrown into the fire and burned. If you remain in me and my words remain in you, ask whatever you wish, and it will be given you. This is to my Father's glory, that you bear much fruit, showing yourselves to be my disciples.

"As the Father has loved me, so have I loved you. Now remain in my love. If you obey my commands, you will remain in my love, just as I have obeyed my Father's commands and remain in his love. I have told you this so that my joy may be in you and that your joy may be complete. My command is this: Love each other as I have loved you. Greater love has no one than this, that he lay down his life for his friends. You are my friends if you do what I command. I no longer call you servants, because a servant does not know his master's business. Instead, I have called you friends, for everything that I learned from my Father I have made known to you. You did not choose me,

but I chose you and appointed you to go and bear fruit—fruit that will last. Then the Father will give you whatever you ask in my name.

*   *   *

2 Peter 1:5-11

For this very reason, make every effort to add to your faith goodness; and to goodness, knowledge; and to knowledge, self-control; and to self-control, perseverance; and to perseverance, godliness; and to godliness, brotherly kindness; and to brotherly kindness, love. For if you possess these qualities in increasing measure, they will keep you from being ineffective and unproductive in your knowledge of our Lord Jesus Christ. But if anyone does not have them, he is nearsighted and blind, and has forgotten that he has been cleansed from his past sins.

Therefore, my brothers, be all the more eager to make your calling and election sure. For if you do these things, you will never fall, and you will receive a rich welcome into the eternal kingdom of our Lord and Savior Jesus Christ.

Luke 15:11-32

Prodigal Sons
UNDERSTANDING THE PARABLE

*Jesus continued: "There was a man who had two sons. The younger
one said to his father, 'Father, give me my share of the estate.' So he
divided his property between them.*

*"Not long after that, the younger son got together all he had, set off
for a distant country and there squandered his wealth in wild living.
After he had spent everything, there was a severe famine in that whole
country, and he began to be in need. So he went and hired himself out
to a citizen of that country, who sent him to his fields to feed pigs. He
longed to fill his stomach with the pods that the pigs were eating, but
no one gave him anything.*

*"When he came to his senses, he said, 'How many of my father's
hired men have food to spare, and here I am starving to death! I will
set out and go back to my father and say to him: Father, I have sinned
against heaven and against you. I am no longer worthy to be called
your son; make me like one of your hired men.' So he got up and went
to his father.*

*"But while he was still a long way off, his father saw him and was
filled with compassion for him; he ran to his son, threw his arms
around him and kissed him.*

"The son said to him, 'Father, I have sinned against heaven and against you. I am no longer worthy to be called your son.'

"But the father said to his servants, 'Quick! Bring the best robe and put it on him. Put a ring on his finger and sandals on his feet. Bring the fattened calf and kill it. Let's have a feast and celebrate. For this son of mine was dead and is alive again; he was lost and is found.' So they began to celebrate.

"Meanwhile, the older son was in the field. When he came near the house, he heard music and dancing. So he called one of the servants and asked him what was going on. 'Your brother has come,' he replied, 'and your father has killed the fattened calf because he has him back safe and sound.'

"The older brother became angry and refused to go in. So his father went out and pleaded with him. But he answered his father, 'Look! All these years I've been slaving for you and never disobeyed your orders. Yet you never gave me even a young goat so I could celebrate with my friends. But when this son of yours who has squandered your property with prostitutes comes home, you kill the fattened calf for him!'

"'My son,' the father said, 'you are always with me, and everything I have is yours. But we had to celebrate and be glad, because this brother of yours was dead and is alive again; he was lost and is found.'" LUKE 15:11-32

Introduction

The parable of the Prodigal Son is one of the two most famous parables Jesus told (the Good Samaritan being the other). Just as the word 'Samaritan' has taken on new meaning as a result of the parable, so too has 'prodigal' come to refer not only to someone who is wasteful (the historic meaning of the word), but also to someone who has left his home and faith, and become lost to his family.

It's not hard to understand why this parable has been a favorite since the early centuries of the church: the picture of a loving father accepting home a wayward son pulls at most people's heartstrings. In fact, this aspect of the parable is so compelling that over time it has overshadowed almost every-thing else. The sentimental side of the story has sometimes made it a challenge to interpret the parable accurately.

But Jesus began the parable with, "There was a man who had two sons"—not one son. The story of the younger, wasteful son takes up only the first part of the parable; the second part concerns the reaction of the older son to his father's actions.

The parable of the so-called Prodigal Son is really a story about *two* lost sons. In it Jesus is comparing and con-trasting two types of lostness, one symbolized by the younger son and one by the older. When we see the parable from this perspective, it takes on a new complexity and addresses two of the major concerns facing those who would enter the Kingdom of God.

Setting and Context

We have mentioned before that Luke records Jesus' journey to Jerusalem to be crucified in chapters 9:51 to 19:44. In chapter 15, Luke tells us, "Now the tax collectors and 'sinners' were all gathering around to hear him. But the Pharisees and the teachers of the law muttered, 'This man welcomes sinners and eats with them.'" (Luke 15:1-2)

According to this introductory passage, two groups had gathered around Jesus to listen to Him teach. The first consisted of tax collectors and sinners, or those Jews who had forsaken God's law publicly. The tax collectors were those who worked for the government taking in taxes; they consistently fleeced the people for more money. It was common practice in those days for tax collectors to mark up taxes and keep the difference for themselves. Sinners could have been any num-ber of people, including prostitutes, drunkards, thieves, and others who outwardly bucked the religious system of the day.

The second group consisted of the Pharisees and teachers of the law. These were the men who attempted to follow the law as perfectly as they knew how. They were very moral men, people who on the outside did exactly what was expected of them. The law was their standard, and although it was a good standard, it had become an end in itself, obscuring their relationships with God.

Jesus identified the Pharisees' basic problem when He told them, "Isaiah was right when he prophesied about you hypocrites; as it is written: 'These people honor me with their lips, but their hearts are far from me. They worship me in vain; their teachings are but rules taught by men.' You have let go of the commands of God and are holding on to the traditions of men." (Mark 7:6-8) For the Pharisees and teachers, anyone who broke the law or traditions was unacceptable in their eyes, *as well as anyone who associated with those law-breakers.*

Hence their distrust of Jesus. Jesus made a point of spending time with public lawbreakers, and the religious leaders didn't like it. To put it in current terms, Jesus spent more time with druggies and street-walkers than He did with church elders and deacons. We might find it a bit disconcerting ourselves if someone did this today — but perhaps that is a sign of our own problems.

With the two groups in front of Him — the immoral and the moral, the lawbreakers and the law-abiders, the unrighteous and the self-righteous — Jesus told three parables. In one respect these parables are aimed primarily at the Pharisees and teachers of the law. After all, they were the ones muttering about those with whom Jesus kept company, those same "lost sheep of Israel" whom it was their duty to take care of. All three parables are about being lost and found, and the public reactions that go with it.

Jesus' first parable is the famous story of the lost sheep that is sought by the shepherd. When the shepherd finds the sheep he brings it home and celebrates with the village over his find. Jesus then explains that the story is about sinners repenting and how heaven rejoices over it. Interestingly enough, the sheep - which is compared to a spiritually lost sinner - never does anything other than become lost. It is the shepherd who does all the positive action in finding and bringing the sheep home. In other words, it is the responsibility of those who are law-abiders to go out and bring in those who are law-break-ers. (It is also an interesting commentary on the true nature of repentance, something normally associated with the action of the repentant. In the first two parables the action of the seeker is much more important than the action of the one who is lost.)

Jesus' second parable is the parable of the lost coin. A woman loses a coin and searches carefully until she finds it. She calls her friends to rejoice and Jesus again draws a comparison between the celebration in the story and the celebration in heaven over a sinner who repents.

These two parables set the stage for Jesus' most impres-sively-designed parable. At every level it is a masterpiece of beauty and teaching, exploring many interrelated themes simultaneously. In light of its relationship to the two preced-ing parables, we assume from the outset that it will be about someone losing something very valuable and seeking it. Yet Jesus again turns the tables on His listeners, for in this last parable someone is lost but no one goes to seek him. In one sense, it is this missing element that is so important for us to note. In its place we find an older brother who brings a whole new perspective to Jesus' specific teaching about being lost.

The Division of Property

There was a man who had two sons. The younger one said to his father, "Father, give me my share of the estate." So he divided his property between them. LUKE 15:11-12

Jesus begins the parable by introducing the three main charac-ters. The father is a wealthy, landed farmer. How do we know he is wealthy? First, the story tells us that he has a fattened

calf on hand (only people of means would have had din-
ner for fifty ready at a moment's notice). We know he has
a number of servants, and although the exact number is not
stated, from those who are mentioned there is the sense that
there are many of them. And, finally, he has enough property to divide so that, once divided, it still provides plenty of
income to support those who are left.

His two sons would have worked on his estate in some
capacity. When we see the older son the second time, he is
returning from the fields. It would have been assumed the
younger son had some estate responsibilities as well, although
his generally wasteful actions could have made people think
he was lazy. A wealthy father with two sons was a very normal
picture in Middle Eastern culture.

The younger son's request for his part of the inheritance,
however, was not. Kenneth Bailey tells us that "in all of Middle
Eastern literature (aside from this parable) from ancient times
to the present, there is no case of any son, older or younger,
asking for his inheritance from a father who is still in good
health."[1] Bailey goes further and explains that culturally such a
request was equal to the son saying, "I wish you were dead."[2] An
audience hearing this story in the ancient Middle East would
expect the father to angrily reject his younger son's request
and throw him out of his presence for being so disrespectful.[3]
It was therefore even more shocking that the father's chooses
to grant the request.

This is the situation we see paralleled in the film *Prodigal
Sons*. Mr. Hawthorne owns a large and prosperous healthcare
company. His two sons work for him. The older son, Andrew, is dedicated to hard work and performance; the younger
son, Jake, spends his days pursuing a more leisurely existence.
Jake decides he wants his share of the company regardless of
the consequences, and asks his father for it. The company's
board recognizes that such a request will not only hurt the

company, but is tantamount to Jake saying he wants his father dead. Nevertheless, Mr. Hawthorne grants his request.

In both the parable and the film, the real issue at stake is that the younger son has a broken relationship with his father. He's more interested in what his father can give him than in having a relationship with him. Furthermore, he cares little for the family as a whole. In the original parable, the father would have had to give the younger son land and animals currently being used by the estate, since that was what his wealth was measured in. Such a loss for a family would have caused much suffering.[4]

In the same way, Jake pulling out his inheritance results in financial trauma for the company. We begin to get a sense of the younger son's selfishness when we realize that even though his actions directly hurt those around him, he cares little for the consequences. He is primarily interested in fulfilling his own desires.

In the parable, Jesus draws a direct comparison between the younger son and the man or woman who has rejected God's law. This is the sinner, the immoral person, the lawbreaker. Such a person is basically selfish, wanting the things God has created more than God Himself, and therefore blatantly rejecting any relationship with Him. The sinner's break with God is a public break. He is saying with his actions that he wants nothing to do with the loving God who created him.

God tells us in many places that He is not pleased with such a choice. Jesus attacked those who were despoiling God's house. He drove out the money changers and their sheep and cattle from the temple because they ultimately cared more about what God's temple could do for them than what they could do for God. (John 2:14-16) Jesus' time spent with sinners consistently resulted in their repentance. It is not as if Jesus went easy on the unrighteous; rather, He came to save them from themselves and told them so: "Stop sinning or something worse may happen to you." (John 5:14) God may allow some people to use His things with impunity for a short time, but as the parable shows us, they eventually ruin themselves by their choices.

The older brother is a different matter. At the start of the parable he is mentioned once, then we hear nothing else from him until the younger son's return. Although his inaction may mean little to us, it spoke volumes to the original audience. In that culture it was expected that the eldest brother would act as mediator between the father and the children who were at odds with him or with one another.[5] We see something similar to this in the Old Testament when Reuben seeks to save Joseph from his brothers and return him to his father. (Gen 37:21-21)

Yet this older son remains silent. In the film, we see the tensions between the older brother and his father when a board member asks Andrew what he said to his brother to convince him he shouldn't do this. His father waits on his answer, but instead of interceding between his father and his brother, he says the company doesn't need Jake. Before this scene, Andrew had said that his brother was a cancer that needed to be cut out. There is clearly no love lost between these two brothers.

In terms of the original parable, this omission on Jesus' part implies that there is something wrong in the relationship between the father and his older son. Their dialogue at the end of the parable confirms this. Whereas the younger son is more interested in what his father can give him, the older son is more interested in controlling his father.

This brings us to the moment of the actual division of the property. Notice that Jesus tells us "he divided his property between *them*." This means the older brother received his share when the younger brother received his. Again, following custom, it would have been expected that the older brother would publicly refuse his share as a statement of the injustice of the action. Yet his quiet acceptance emphasizes his own problems in his relationship with his father.[6]

Bailey brings up one more important distinction in the original culture concerning the nature of inheritance and the right of *possession* versus the right of *disposition*. The former meant that one was entitled to the inheritance but might not have control over it to do what one wanted with it. It would have been possible for someone to give the inheritance to someone (right of possession) but still maintain control over it (right of disposition).[7]

In the younger son's instance, he is given both rights since we see him selling off the property in the next verse. As far as the older son goes, the father's comments at the end of the story imply that the older son has the right of possession due to the division ("everything I have is yours…") but had not asked for the right of disposition ("you never gave me even a young goat…," implying that he does not have complete control over everything). This distinction is helpful to understand as we move into the next part of the story.

The First Lost Son

Not long after that, the younger son got together all he had, set off for a distant country and there squandered his wealth in wild living.
LUKE 15:13

As we pointed out earlier, in the original parable the father's wealth would have been measured in property and animals. Such things are not very portable. The younger son needed to sell off the family lands and livestock in order to get cash to take with him. That is what Jesus meant when He said that the younger son "got together all he had."

Such lands would have been in the family for generations. To the original audience, ancestral lands would have had a sense of sacredness to them. The land was a gift from God to the people; the son's complete disregard of his ancestral responsibilities is therefore another sign of his disregard for authority and tradition. The local village would have found his actions detestable, just as Mr. Hawthorne's board finds Jakes actions unconscionable.[8]

Nevertheless, the younger son goes through with his plan. He takes his money and goes off to a distant country. Such a country would have been occupied by gentiles or foreigners; that is, non-Jews whose religion and cultural practices were unacceptable according to Biblical religion. This was not simply a sense of racial and religious pride. God Himself had separated His people from foreigners and put strong cultural boundaries between them. Although Jesus would eventually break down those barriers, during the time of their use they served an important purpose in keeping the people of God holy and distinct from idolatrous nations. In Jesus' day gentiles were idol worshipers, and any foreign land the younger son would travel to would have been filled with gentiles. In other words, he was physically separating himself from what he knew to be true.

As a comparison, to many people living in the heartland of the United States, New York City can seem like a foreign land. It appears to operate on different principles and at a different speed from the rest of the country. It is a city where great wealth is amassed and lost on a daily basis, and which can seem less traditional and moral than other parts of the country. In the film, Jake's departure for New York City parallels the younger son's departure for a foreign land.

Jesus tells us that there the younger son "squandered his wealth in wild living." The Greek word used for wild living does not necessarily imply either moral or immoral living, but rather being wasteful with his money.[9] In spite of that, the older brother's charge at the end of parable that he wasted his money with prostitutes has influenced many interpretations of this verse.

But there are a number of problems with reading the older brother's comment earlier into the story, not the least of which is that *the older brother wasn't there.* As we will see when we get to that part of the parable, this accusation is much more malicious than it may appear on the surface. Even further, Kenneth Bailey tells us that most of the Middle Eastern translations of the text do not condemn the younger son for immorality but rather translate the words as being "luxurious" and "wasteful" – an important distinction.[10] These cultures see his wastefulness as parties, gifts, and personal luxury. Such excess forms a sharp contrast to what lies in store for him.

This is what we see in our film. Jake spends money with no thought for the future. He has so much it seems he can't run out. The amounts that Andrew calculates show both the size and speed with which Jake spends – something very realistic in New York City. Jake throws away his father's fortune on pleasures and thinks nothing of it.

Even though he was wealthy, the younger son was certainly not productive. He lived off his father's hard work and provisions, thinking little of where it came from and even less of what the future held. Like many sinners today, he was living off resources that were never meant to be used that way and would one day suddenly run out.

The Great Loss

> *After he had spent everything, there was a severe famine in that whole country, and he began to be in need. So he went and hired himself out to a citizen of that country, who sent him to his fields to feed pigs. He longed to fill his stomach with the pods that the pigs were eating, but no one gave him anything.* LUKE 15:14-16

In the ancient world there were few things more devastating to a community than a famine. Famines usually resulted from seasons of bad crops and would quickly constrict the food

supply of a nation. The most famous famine in the Bible is
the one before which Joseph stored up grain for seven years,
then sold it back to the Egyptians, saving them and the surrounding peoples from starvation.

The younger son stands in stark contrast to Joseph. His
wanton wastefulness has exposed him to a catastrophe that
could even take his life. There was no state welfare in those
days and no unemployment. He was a Jew living amongst gentiles so he could not turn to strangers and expect them to help
him, as he could if he were still living in his own country.

In his distress he takes a job. In times of famine, there
would have been countless needy people in the community.
The closest approximation we can come to in the modern
West is an economic recession or depression where many
people are out of work and it's difficult for them to purchase
the things they need to live on. In the same way, there would
have been many people needing work.

It is therefore curious that this citizen offers him a job
feeding pigs. Pigs were considered ceremonially unclean by
Jews, something that would have been known by people in
the countries around Israel. It is a disgusting job for a Jew
because he is in constant association with that which he was
brought up to detest. Could it be that the citizen was offering
him a job he expected him to reject, almost taunting him with
such a position?[11] As our film shows us, cleaning up around
dead bodies is a job that would disgust most people. It's important to realize that just the idea of feeding pigs would turn
the stomachs of the first-century Jewish audience.

That the younger son accepts the job shows how bad
things are. To emphasize this further, Jesus says that he is so
hungry he wants the same food the pigs are eating. Yet no one
is looking out for him. No one cares that he is there dying of
starvation. He is on his own, separated totally from his family.
No one is coming to look for him.

Let us now bring up what is missing in comparison be-

tween this parable and the two parables preceding it. In both
the other parables someone goes out to look for what is lost,
finds it, and then brings it home. Who in this parable should
be the one to go out and look for the younger brother and
bring him home?

Is it not the older brother? Yet unlike the shepherd and
the woman, both of whom consider what was lost to be very valuable and take great strides to find it again, we know that the older
brother has nothing but anger and contempt for his younger
sibling. This "missing searcher" is important to remember.
We will discuss it again when we come to the older brother's
dialogue with his father.

Gutter Sensibility

> *When he came to his senses, he said, "How many of my father's hired*
> *men have food to spare, and here I am starving to death! I will set out*
> *and go back to my father and say to him: Father, I have sinned against*
> *heaven and against you. I am no longer worthy to be called your son;*
> *make me like one of your hired men." So he got up and went to his*
> *father.* LUKE 15:17-20

It's amazing how the gutter can put one's life in an entirely
new perspective. This brings up an interesting question: was
the younger son suddenly showing a repentant heart? Luke
uses the phrase "he came to himself" instead of the traditional
word for repentance which he uses approximately twenty-five
times both in his gospel and the book of Acts. Instead of true
repentance, this appears to be a change of mind based on circumstances rather than a true change of heart. [12] The younger
son is lamenting the pain of his bad condition rather than the
pain he's caused his father through his choices.

This comes out even more pointedly when he hatches a
plan intended to get him home. His father's hired men have
much more than he does. He can go tell his father that it's his

fault ("I have sinned against heaven and against you"), that he should not receive the benefits of sonship ("I am no longer worthy to be called your son"); and that he could become like one of his hired men.

Yet let's look for a moment at this position of a "hired man." Kenneth Bailey tells us there were three levels of servants on a first-century estate: 1) Bondsmen, or slaves who were part of the estate; 2) Slaves of a lower class than bondsmen; and 3) hired servants, or men who had no part in the estate but were hired on a daily basis.[13] In other words, the younger son wants to be in this last category, a free person, independent of his father, but able to work and earn an income. Furthermore, in this capacity he could work and try to pay back some of what he owed his father.

This plan has a number of positive points for the younger son. First, he can maintain his sense of pride that even though he lost everything, he can still work and have a job. Second, he will not be under his older brother's authority. After all, his older brother owns what is left of the estate.[14]

In the film, this is the same situation in which we find Jake. He daily sees the hospital administrators in the building, knows his father hires the same type of men, and thinks that he could do that, too, if just given a chance. He could apologize to his father for all he's lost (he realizes he has to say *something* about losing all that money), then tell him that he can work as a manager in one of his hospitals. It's a bit of a crazy scheme, as his friend reminds him, but the younger son knows he has to do something to change his situation.

This does not appear to be the thinking of true repentance. Instead, the younger son appears to be motivated by self-preservation, and if there is some regret in his thinking it is overshadowed by his need to take care of himself. True repentance would not seek his own security but would address the primary problem: his relationship with his father.

Nevertheless, with his plan formulated in his mind, he heads back to his father.

The Gracious Homecoming

But while he was still a long way off, his father saw him and was filled with compassion for him; he ran to his son, threw his arms around him and kissed him. The son said to him, "Father, I have sinned against heaven and against you. I am no longer worthy to be called your son." But the father said to his servants, "Quick! Bring the best robe and put it on him. Put a ring on his finger and sandals on his feet. Bring the fattened calf and kill it. Let's have a feast and celebrate. For this son of mine was dead and is alive again; he was lost and is found." So they began to celebrate. LUKE 15:20-24

If the parable of the prodigal son is the most famous of Jesus' parables, then this part of the story is the most well-loved. Over time, commentators and pastors have painted the picture of a lonely father pining away for his son, waiting every day by the window to see if he's coming home. It is a lovely picture.

The problem is, the text says nothing about it. Instead, it says that the father sees the son while he was still a long way off. In a land of gently rolling hills and fields (such as Galilee) it would have been easy for him to see him while in the distance. But the parable doesn't say he was waiting for him to show up.

Jesus' point in having the father see the son in the distance is that it gives the father the opportunity *to go to him*. This is what is so extraordinary and what is sometimes obscured by the sentimentality of a waiting father. Dignified, wealthy men do not go out to meet wayward sons; rather, wayward sons go in to repent before them. [15] And if they ever do go out of their homes, they certainly don't run: it is a degrading thing to do. [16]

Why does the father respond this way? Jesus tells us that when the father saw his son, he felt *compassion* for him. This is the same word that Luke uses to describe the emotions of the Samaritan for the man in need. It is a deep and abiding love that moves to action. [17]

The first thing the father does when he sees his son is to throw his arms around him and kiss him. These kisses are signs both to his son and to the watching community that he is forgiving his son and reconciling him to himself.[18] It is not difficult to imagine what had been going through the son's head before he sees the father: rehearsing his speech, fearing the meeting, wondering what he would say, seeing the community draw around him as he came into the village. The father's reaction would certainly surprise him.

The son gives his prepared speech, but "make me like one of your hired men" is strangely missing. It is too obvious an omission in such a short story to have been accidental (see endnote for a different view on this omission).[19] Rather, it is a sign that the son has come to a true level of repentance. He has sinned against his father and isn't worthy to be called his son *but* he's not going to try to work his way back into good standing.[20]

Why this change of heart? It is because of the father's unexpected outpouring of love and demonstration of humility *in spite of what the younger son had done.* The father's compassion brought the younger son to a place of true repentance. Prior to this, his coming to his senses was based on his painful situation. His coming to repentance is based on his father's love.

It is an important distinction. The father's affection precedes any confession. In theological terms, grace always precedes true repentance. After all, in his speech the younger son never gets past "I'm not worthy." In the first draft, he felt he was worthy to do something to earn back his father's favor; he intended to tell his father to give him a job. After his father's outpouring of love he recognizes that it was never about the money and always about his relationship to his father.

The father's response confirms this. He gives four orders which would have had great significance to the original audience. First, he tells his servants to dress his returned son in the best robe. The best robe would have been the father's robe, used for feast days. Anyone in the village who looked at him would know immediately he had been reaccepted into the family. The ring would be the signet ring, a sign that he has authority to do business for the estate; in other words, he is giving him back his job as a ruling member of the family. The sandals are the sign of being free and not a servant, thus reestablishing the son's authority over the servants who put them on his feet.[21]

Finally, he tells the servants to kill the fattened calf and prepare for a feast to celebrate. A fattened calf would take months of feeding and care; it was an expensive luxury. In light of the lack of refrigeration in those days, when an animal was killed it was expected to be eaten soon after. This large amount of meat would have been enough to feed a very large gathering of people, far beyond the immediate household.[22] The father not only expects to celebrate with his family, but for the entire village to join them. He explains why: "For this son of mine was dead and is alive again; he was lost and is found."

There is a clear parallel in the father's language here and the language of the shepherd and the woman in the preceding parables. There is joy and excitement over finding what was lost to them and the natural thing to do is celebrate.

Jesus provides the spiritual significance of this banquet when He says in the two preceding parables that "there is rejoicing in the presence of the angels of God over one sinner who repents." (Luke 15:10) These three parables come as a sequence concerning the lost, so this interpretation naturally holds for the current parable as well. The parallels between the natural and spiritual realms show us that if the earthly servants are like angels, then the father in the story is a picture of God in heaven. The picture of the eschatological banquet at the end of time is strong in the New Testament, and a number of scholars see overtones of the final banquet in this banquet for the lost son. Everyone is overjoyed at the son's return.

Everyone, that is, but the older brother.

The Second Lost Son

> *Meanwhile, the older son was in the field. When he came near the house, he heard music and dancing. So he called one of the servants and asked him what was going on. "Your brother has come," he replied, "and your father has killed the fattened calf because he has him back safe and sound." The older brother became angry and refused to go in. So his father went out and pleaded with him. But he answered his father, "Look! All these years I've been slaving for you and never disobeyed your orders. Yet you never gave me even a young goat so I could celebrate with my friends. But when this son of yours who has squandered your property with prostitutes comes home, you kill the fattened calf for him!"* LUKE 15:25-30

The second half of the parable begins with the older son returning from work. It is an appropriate re-introduction to someone who sees merit as the basis of his relationship with his father. Just as in the film, the older son is surprised and curious as to the meaning of the festivities. But his curiosity turns quickly to anger. It doesn't matter to him that the reason for the celebration is that his younger brother is safe. His response shows that he doesn't care whether his brother is dead or alive.

The older brother's angry reaction serves as the first point of contrast between him and the two other seekers in the preceding parables. Where they experience joy and excitement, he experiences anger and frustration. Not only was it the older brother's responsibility to seek the lost, it should have been his loving, filial desire. Yet he cares nothing for his lost brother. Even further, his real interest is in the financial matters at stake. The issue of killing the fattened calf becomes the prevailing theme of the older son's repugnance. He latches onto it for a number of reasons, not the least of which is that he is now the owner of it.

And so he refuses to go into the party and welcome his brother home. To the original audience, this would have been a highly disrespectful gesture from the older son to his father. In a family gathering, the older son had responsibility to act as the host to the guests, greeting them, offering them more food, and ordering the servants to meet the guests' needs.[23] He would have been expected to go in immediately and welcome home his brother, hiding his personal disgust in deference to his father's pleasure.

But the older son doesn't care about his relationship with his father. There is a striking parallel between the two sons here: both evidence the same kind of pride in their particular positions. Both are selfish in their own particular ways. Both are lost to the father.

So the father goes out to him. Such an action would have halted the party since the most important person was leaving the table and going out to see his angry son. The son's actions are publicly insulting to the father, literally humiliating him in front of his guests. In Middle Eastern culture, this kind of behavior was an enormous insult.[24] Yet the father's love for his sons includes accepting the humiliation that results from their rejection. If there is any underlying theme in this parable, it is that the father is consistently gracious toward sons who do not deserve it.

In the original culture, the expected reaction of the father would have been anger. He should have demanded that his son go into the party. Yet again, this father does not react like any father the culture had ever seen. As his guests watch, the father pleads with his son to come into the party and welcome home his brother. Where he has every right to demand, he instead reasons with him.

It is here that the parable starts to explore the inner workings of the self-righteous heart. Prior to this it examined the highs and lows of the sinner's choices that led him back to

God and His transforming grace. Now it focuses on the attitude of the self-righteous man who is trying to follow God's law, yet in reality is far from knowing God.

The older son's contempt is evident in his first words. Whereas previously in the parable the younger son always addressed his father with his proper title, the older son gives him an order, again emphasizing his disrespect for him.[25] He draws a contrast between himself and his younger brother by saying "all these years..." Although we don't know exactly how long the younger brother was gone, this implies that he had been gone for some time, and is a reminder to the father that *he* was not the one who had abandoned the family.

The older son goes on to say how he has been "slaving" away for the father during that time. But this is an odd perspective for a son who essentially possesses the entire estate. A slave occupied the lowest position in ancient society and worked not by choice but by requirement. The older son is saying that he views himself as a slave: but why is that? Is it possible that a life based only on law-keeping encourages a slave mentality in those who pursue it?

From this point forward his argument begins to lose touch with reality. He says he never disobeyed his father's orders yet he's disobeying him at that very moment, publicly insulting him before the entire community. In the film, Andrew's narrative begins to falter near the end of the story when he assumes his brother wouldn't take a job (he does) and that his father really doesn't have any authority anymore (he does). The issue here is that the self-righteous man begins to define his own actions and the world around him according to his own warped perspective.

But that is not the only issue. As he looks at the world through his own law-based worldview, he comes to doubt that his father really loves him. This is the meaning of "you never gave me even a young goat so I could celebrate with my friends." In terms of value, a young goat was a commonplace animal and worth far less than a fattened calf. In other words, *you love him more than you love me since you never gave me even a fraction of what you've given him.* It is a childish statement that reveals the deep sense of insecurity about his position in the family. He is basically unsure of his father's love for him.

Furthermore, he doesn't understand the true nature of celebration. To be fair, the younger son also didn't understand it for a time. There are three types of festivities mentioned in this parable: the first is the assumed wasteful, extravagant parties of the younger son; the second is the true celebration of the father; and the third is this trumped up get-together with friends of the older son. Notice how the first and the third have selfishness as their root, while the second is motivated by joy. There is a sour note to the older son's idea of a celebration that is more similar to the younger son's party than the father's: neither the younger nor the older son wanted to celebrate *with* their family; rather, their mistaken idea of celebration is with those *outside* their family. Symbolically this suggests that neither the sinner nor the self-righteous are interested in the true messianic, familial banquet of God. It is the acceptance of God's grace that brings the sinner into the celebration, but the self-righteous man fights against it.

The older son soon turns vitriolic against both the younger son and the father. Instead of saying "my brother" he refers to him as "this son of yours," essentially denying any relationship to his brother, something his inaction to seek him demonstrated much earlier. It is another slap in the face to his father, reminding him publicly – remember, everyone is listening to this – how his brother lost all his money.

His story takes yet another turn for the worse when he says that his brother lost it with "prostitutes." Arland Hultgren points out that this translation is not quite strong enough but that a more shocking word like "whores" is more accurate for a public outburst.[26] But where does the older brother get this?

He doesn't know what his younger brother was doing all that time he was away. All he knows is that he came back without any money. It is an ugly accusation that seeks to degrade his younger brother before his father and the community.

His disgust finally resolves itself in his bitter statement concerning the fattened calf. The older son is ultimately just as concerned about money as the younger son. He's basically saying "you wasted your own money on him, and now you're wasting *my* money on him with this fattened calf." The older son wants to control the father's actions, denying grace and love to those he feels are not deserving. The younger brother had rejected the older brother's world of merit and work, so he should be rejected entirely from the family. The older brother sees himself as the exact opposite of his younger sibling.

Yet, in terms of being lost from a relationship with their father, they are remarkably alike. Kenneth Bailey quotes Ibrahim Sa'id, an Egyptian Christian scholar, saying, "The difference between [the older brother] and his younger brother is that the younger brother was estranged and rebellious while absent from the house, but the older son was estranged and rebellious in his heart while he was in the house. The estrangement and rebellion of the younger son were evident in his surrender to his passions and in his request to leave his father's house. The estrangement and rebellion of the older son were evident in his anger and his refusal to enter the house."[27]

Sadly, the older son is blinded by his own self-righteousness and the judgment of those around him to seeing his own condition. Yet his father continues to reach out to him.

The Father's Grace

> *"My son," the father said, "you are always with me, and everything I have is yours. But we had to celebrate and be glad, because this brother of yours was dead and is alive again; he was lost and is found."* LUKE 15:31-32

In spite of his son's response, his father speaks tenderly to him. Where the older son refuses to use the appropriate title, his father gently talks to him using the possessive "my son." He affirms his hard work and his steadfastness to the family when he says "you are always with me." Yet there is a double sense here: it can refer to the fact that he has been with him working, but it can also be a question that asks "how can you have been so physically close, yet remained so emotionally distant?"

His father also affirms that that the older brother owns the rest of the estate. Yet he wants to teach his son the true reason behind the celebration: the redemption of his lost brother. It is not a matter of favoritism or exploitation, but the simple fact that someone who was dead to the family is now alive to them again. Such a return *requires* that there be a celebration according to the law of love.

Yet this is a law that the older son does not understand. It is a law that the self-righteous man does not comprehend, primarily because love toward his father is lacking in his heart. He can only love himself.

Here ends the parable. But there is a final dramatic beat that is missing. The entire second half of the parable has been structured to arrive at a situation that does not come.[28] The literary structure of the narrative reveals that Jesus is pressing those who are listening to want the older son to go into the feast, yet Jesus does not provide the final narrative step. As a result, His listeners must remain in that moment of tension, deciding for themselves what *they* should do.

It is clear that Jesus means for this decision to haunt the Pharisees and experts in the law. It is not difficult to see how the points of comparison line up: the sinners and tax collectors are like the younger son, flagrantly disobeying God's laws but returning in repentant humility to God; God is like the father, graciously going out to meet His lost children whether they are sinners or self-righteous; and the Pharisees are like the older brother, always doing what they feel should be done, yet still as lost from the father's love as their brothers. *Even more so, they are potentially rejecting the grace that God is extending to them through Jesus Christ.*

This parable is not only a warning, it is also a condemnation. When compared to the preceding two parables, it is a reminder to those who know the law that it is their responsibility to go out and graciously bring in those who have rejected it. But instead of supporting Jesus in His ministry to the lost sheep of Israel, the Pharisees and teachers of the law denounced Him for His actions. In return, Jesus condemned them for their hypocrisy, saying "Woe to you, teachers of the law and Pharisees, you hypocrites! You shut the kingdom of heaven in men's faces. You yourselves do not enter, nor will you let those enter who are trying to.... On the outside you appear to people as righteous but on the inside you are full of hypocrisy and wickedness." (Matt 23:13, 28)

This parable's lack of a character who goes out and searches for the lost son is not intended to imply that God does not go out and seek lost sinners; the two preceding parables showed that this is exactly what He does. Rather, this particular parable was constructed to show what was lacking in both brothers—and to show that the father goes out to meet both of them where they are spiritually. Furthermore, it was intended to convict those in the religious leadership who cared little for their flock who were lost all around them.

Summary

In closing, we see that the parable of the prodigal son might be better named the parable of the two lost sons. In it Jesus compares two kinds of lostness: that of the law-breaking sinner and that of the law-abiding self-righteous. Neither son desires to have a relationship with the father and both are lost in their own prideful selfishness. The father in this story, symbolizing God, shows grace to both sinners and self-righteous alike through the work of His son Jesus. Yet that grace was being rejected by the Pharisees and teachers of the law on a daily basis. The parable forces them to grapple with their own reaction to Jesus, as well as their attitudes toward their fellow Jews who had rejected God's law. Jesus is encouraging the self-righteous man to look at himself and his actions in light of God's calling.

PARALLELS

ORIGINAL PARABLE	PARABLE FILM
The father is a wealthy landowner.	Mr. Hawthorne, the father, is a wealthy owner of a company.
He has two sons who work on the family estate.	He has two sons who work for the family company.
Younger son asks for his share of the estate.	Jake, the younger son, asks for his share of the company.
The younger son asking for his inheritance while his father is still alive is like saying, "I want you dead."	Jake asking for his inheritance while his father is still alive is like saying, "I want you dead."
Older brother is expected to intercede as peacemaker between the father and younger son, but does nothing.	Andrew, the older brother, is expected to intercede as peacemaker between the father and younger son, but does nothing.
Father divides his property between his two sons.	Mr. Hawthorne divides his ownership in the company between his two sons.
Younger son sells off the family property for cash.	Jake cashes out his ownership in the company.
Younger son leaves for a gentile country, far from home both geographically and morally.	Jake leaves for New York City, far from home geographically and morally.

Younger son wastes his money by lavish spending on his friends and on himself.	Jake wastes his money by lavish spending on expensive cars, apartments, and lifestyle.
Younger son spends all his money.	Jake spends all his money.
There was a severe famine in the country.	There is a severe recession in the country.
Younger son is broke.	Jake is broke.
Younger son finds a job with a gentile farmer.	Jake finds a job with a hospital hiring manager.
The gentile farmer gives him a job feeding pigs, a detestable job for Jews.	The hiring manager gives him a job helping out in the morgue, a detestable job for most people.
He was hungry and wanted to eat what the pigs were eating, but no one gave him anything.	Jake is out of money, but no one cares for him in his situation.
He comes to his senses working with the pigs and realizes the true nature of his situation.	Jake comes to his senses working in the hospital and realizes the true nature of his situation.
He thinks about his father's hired men and how well they are taken care of in comparison to his situation.	Jake sees the hospital administrators and thinks about the men his father hires, and how well they are taken care of in comparison to his situation.
The younger son reflects on his bad situation and it motivates him to return to his father.	Jake reflects on his bad situation and it motivates him to return to his father.

The younger son realizes he has forfeited the right to be a son, but thinks he can still make a living by being a skilled artisan (instead of either an owner or a servant).	Jake realizes he has forfeited the right to be a son, but thinks he can still make a living by being a hospital administrator (instead of either an owner or an hourly worker).
He returns to his father, traveling a long distance.	He returns to his father, traveling a long distance.
His father sees his younger son while still a long way off, and before he sees his father.	Mr. Hawthorne sees Jake while he is coming toward him, and before Jake sees him.
His father feels great love for him when he sees him and runs to meet him, disregarding what others think of such an unexpected and undignified response.	Mr. Hawthorne feels great love for him when he sees him and runs to meet him, disregarding what others think of such an unexpected and undignified response.
His father hugs and kisses him before his younger son can give his speech.	Mr. Hawthorne hugs and kisses Jake before he can get out his speech.
The younger son tells his father he's sinned and that he's no longer worthy to be his son, but leaves off the request to be made a skilled artisan – signs that he has reached true repentance.	Jake tells his father he's sorry and that he's no longer worthy to be his son, but leaves off the request to be made a hospital administrator – signs he has reached true repentance.
The father tells his servants to dress him with the finest robe and put a ring on his finger and sandals on his feet – all signs that he has been completely reaccepted and re-instated to the family.	Mr. Hawthorne tells his secretary to call the board to welcome him back and to clean out his office – all signs that he has been completely reaccepted and re-instated to the family business.

The father tells his servants to bring the fattened calf and kill it, and to have a feast and celebrate in order to show the community his son has been reaccepted as well as to celebrate his return.

Mr. Hawthorne tells his secretary to hire the best restaurant to provide the best food for a party in order to show the company that his son has been reaccepted as well as to celebrate his return.

The older son was in the field working.

Andrew, the older son, was away from the office working.

When the older son comes back into the office he hears music and dancing, and is curious as to what is happening.

When Andrew comes into the office he sees the party and is curious as to what is happening.

One of the servants tells him what has happened.

His father's secretary tells him what has happened.

The older brother becomes angry and refuses to go into the party - a sign of contempt for his brother and disrespect to his father.

Andrew becomes angry and refuses to greet his brother and reaccept - a sign of contempt for his brother and disrespect to his father.

The father goes out and pleads with him to come in.

Mr. Hawthorne goes out and talks gently to him to come in.

The older brother speaks to his father harshly and complains that he's been treated unfairly.

Andrew speaks to his father harshly and complains that he's been treated unfairly.

The older brother argues that his father does not really love him because he hasn't thrown him a party.

Andrew argues that his father does not really love him because he hasn't thrown him a party.

The older son reminds his father that the younger son has lost his money, then says he lost it with prostitutes, a shocking, slanderous statement that he has no proof of.

Andrew reminds his father that the younger son has lost his money, then says that he wasted it on drugs and whores, a shocking, slanderous statement that he has no proof of.

The older son implies that the father is wasting more money on his younger son who first squandered his property and now is the cause behind losing the fattened calf, an expensive piece of property.	Andrew says that Mr. Hawthorne wasting more money on Jake who first squandered his property and now is the cause behind losing all the money spent on the expensive party.
In spite of his older son's anger, the father answers him gently.	In spite of Andrew's anger, Mr. Hawthorne answers him gently.
The father reminds his son that everything he has is his since he divided his estate with him.	Mr. Hawthorne reminds Andrew that everything he has is his since he divided the company between them.
The father encourages his older son to celebrate and be glad because his brother was lost and is now found.	Mr. Hawthorne encourages his older son to celebrate and be glad because his brother was lost and is now found.
We are left wondering what the older son chooses to do.	We are left wondering what Andrew chooses to do.

Endnotes

1 Kenneth Bailey, *Poet & Peasant* (Eerdmans, 1976), 164.

2 Arland J. Hultgren, *The Parables of Jesus* (Eerdmans, 2000), 73.

3 Bailey, *Poet*, 161-162.

4 Kenneth Bailey, *The Cross & the Prodigal* (InterVarsity Press, 2005), 42.

5 Bailey, *Cross*, 45.

6 Bailey, *Poet*, 164.

7 Ibid.

8 Ibid, 169.

9 Hultgren, *Parables*, 75.

10 Bailey, *Poet*, 170.

11 Bailey, *Cross*, 57.

12 Hultgren, *Parables*, 76.

13 Bailey, *Poet*, 176.

14 Ibid, 178.

15 Hultgren, *Parables*, 78.

16 Bailey, *Poet*, 181.

17 Ibid. Hultgren goes on to point out that the term for having compassion occurs a dozen times in the NT, and outside its use in the parables (3 times), it always refers to the divine compassion of Christ.

18 Bailey, *Poet*, 182.

19 It is important to note that many interpreters see the omission of the third part of the speech not as a result of the son's thinking, but as a result of being interrupted by his father. These include such noted scholars as Craig Blomberg and Arland Hultgren, among others. After weighing this as a possibility, this study has chosen to follow the exegesis of Kenneth Bailey as explained in *Poet & Peasant*, pages 183-184.

20 Ibid, 183-184.

21 Ibid, 185.

22 Hultgren, *Parables*, 80.

23 Bailey, *Poet*, 194.

24 Ibid, 195.

25 Ibid, 196.

26 Hultgren, *Parables*, 81.

27 Bailey, *Poet*, 197.

28 Ibid, 191.

Luke 15:11–32

Prodigal Sons
LIVING THE PARABLE

Jesus continued: "There was a man who had two sons. The younger one said to his father, 'Father, give me my share of the estate.' So he divided his property between them.

"Not long after that, the younger son got together all he had, set off for a distant country and there squandered his wealth in wild living. After he had spent everything, there was a severe famine in that whole country, and he began to be in need. So he went and hired himself out to a citizen of that country, who sent him to his fields to feed pigs. He longed to fill his stomach with the pods that the pigs were eating, but no one gave him anything.

"When he came to his senses, he said, 'How many of my father's hired men have food to spare, and here I am starving to death! I will set out and go back to my father and say to him: Father, I have sinned against heaven and against you. I am no longer worthy to be called your son; make me like one of your hired men.' So he got up and went to his father.

"But while he was still a long way off, his father saw him and was filled with compassion for him; he ran to his son, threw his arms around him and kissed him.

"The son said to him, 'Father, I have sinned against heaven and against you. I am no longer worthy to be called your son.'

"But the father said to his servants, 'Quick! Bring the best robe and put it on him. Put a ring on his finger and sandals on his feet. Bring the fattened calf and kill it. Let's have a feast and celebrate. For this son of mine was dead and is alive again; he was lost and is found.' So they began to celebrate.

"Meanwhile, the older son was in the field. When he came near the house, he heard music and dancing. So he called one of the servants and asked him what was going on. 'Your brother has come,' he replied, 'and your father has killed the fattened calf because he has him back safe and sound.'

"The older brother became angry and refused to go in. So his father went out and pleaded with him. But he answered his father, 'Look! All these years I've been slaving for you and never disobeyed your orders. Yet you never gave me even a young goat so I could celebrate with my friends. But when this son of yours who has squandered your property with prostitutes comes home, you kill the fattened calf for him!'

"'My son,' the father said, 'you are always with me, and everything I have is yours. But we had to celebrate and be glad, because this brother of yours was dead and is alive again; he was lost and is found.'" LUKE 15:11-32

TRANSCRIPT OF APPLICATION VIDEO

Living out Prodigal Sons – Rev. Scotty Smith

Rev. Scotty Smith is Founding Pastor of Christ Community Church in Franklin, Tennessee.

Introduction

Without a doubt this is the most beloved and well known of the parables Jesus told. We call it the parable of the prodigal son. It's a sentimental story, and yet we've missed something very vital. Jesus, in introducing this parable, referred to a father having *two* sons. This isn't just the parable of the prodigal son, this is the story of two sons—both of them lost, both of them prodigals, both of them needing equally what a gracious, loving, merciful father alone can give.

Two Types of Lost People

My friend Tim Keller has opened up this parable to a lot of us. He shows that to understand these two sons in the parable is to understand two entirely different ways people deal with God. We can try to relate to God through our own efforts or through trying to run from Him. I know that sounds odd, but there are two ways of dealing with God in our life: as sinners or as the self-righteous. Tax collectors, who were in the community that Jesus was speaking to, and Pharisees and scribes, who were bound up with thinking they could make life work by simply doing it right.

In our day we would give a new language to these two groups: relativists and moralists. The relativist is like the younger brother, really interpreting all of life in his own terms, based upon his own story. The moralist is someone that would reduce the Law of God to rules and regulations. "I think I can put God in the dock, expecting to get from Him what my moralism and obedience deserve." Both of these — the relativist and the moralist — are equally far from the center. Both are just as lost.

The Relativist

Let's talk about the relativist first—the younger brother in our parable. What makes his world tick? How do we understand it? How do we get within his grid? Truth and traditional morality for the younger brother are thrown out the window. That is, at least truth that is objective to me. The younger brother doesn't want someone superimposing a worldview on him. Morality becomes whatever will give me pleasure and meaning – "I don't mean to harm you, but I will be fulfilled."

This is so because, for the younger brother, really the core values of life are personal peace, affluence, pleasure, fulfillment—it really is about me after all. Truly, the younger brother, if he wants the knowledge of God, it's not to know a God to serve and to love, but simply the benefits from whatever worldview, from whatever God will give him what he thinks he must have in order to make life meaningful. It's just about him.

The Moralist

The moralist is the flip side of the coin. He's the older brother in the parable. He embraces traditional morality. He wants to know what the status quo is. He's conservative, he's going to find the mainstream and camp out there. Duty is his mantra and the measure of all things. All of life is reduced down to how I perform, how *you* perform and, tragically, how God performs.

This older brother doesn't obey God because he loves God. He doesn't obey God because of any profound sense in his own heart that God loves him. He obeys God because he wants to control God. He wants a predictable deity—that's why he's reduced the entirety of the Christian life down to tit-for-tat spirituality. I do my part, God must do His part. I do big obedience, God has to bless me. If I fail, it's okay – I can work my way right back because I'm good enough. The moralist stumbles over his own goodness. The bottom line is this – the moralist, the older brother in our midst, really doesn't want to know God any more than the relativist does.

Aspects of Younger Brothers

What do these two brothers have in common, these two sons? They're both lost. They're both disconnected from their own hearts and from the heart of God.

But let's think about the younger brother in particular. What are some of the common themes you will find in younger brothers? Younger brothers are usually outside the church, whether they are un-churched, wanting nothing to do with it, or whether they've de-churched—simply gotten fed up and left. Even if they're hiding out in the church, you will usually find that younger brother distanced from the church in some way.

Younger brothers, because they want to have a free conscience, will minimize, marginalize, or just relativize God's Law. And they do this sometimes by feigning agnosticism or talking about some sort of intellectual problem with God—anything they can do to give their core values—freedom and personal fulfillment—highest priority. They relativize God's Law.

And in time, because they are a law unto themselves, the consequences of living like this catches up to them, leaving them in the gutter metaphorically, literally, spiritually, and physically. More often than not, these younger brothers will come to the end of themselves living out that party dream, but finding out that people leave the party when they run out of the supply.

Aspects of Older Brothers

The truth is, the older brother is just as lost. In fact, his lostness is even more troubling because he's lost in his goodness. He's embraced the Law of God, but it hasn't penetrated his heart—his heart is really not engaged at all. Duty is an end in and of itself for him. Not delighting in the things of God, his goal is not to know God—he wants to predict God. He wants to control God.

Older brothers are hard to discern within the body of Christ because of their goodness. They're spouting the Bible, they're at church when the doors are open, they're having quiet times—and yet there's a smugness, something about them that makes it hard to know what they really are up to. Tragically, what they are not up to is knowing God.

Recognizing Older Brothers

In the church, most of us are not younger brothers—there are
younger brothers in our midst, but there are a lot more older
brothers than we care to admit. How do we recognize these
older brothers?

A joyless, mechanical obedience. Obedience is there, at
least externally—but no joy for the younger brothers who do
find their way home. Indeed, these older brothers, you know
them: the raised eyebrow, the sense of looking down, a disdain towards the weak ones and broken ones in our midst.

That lack of compassion marks the older brother—that
disdain, that smugness. And really what's behind all of that?
More than anything else, the older brother is marked by a lack
of assurance that the Father really loves him or her. How else
can we explain the callousness, the smugness, and the self-
righteous judgmental critical attitude of those who sit in our
churches today except that they are not convinced that the Father loves them as much as He says He does?

Anger stands out as one of the marks of the older brother—
an attitude of heart that says, "God, you owe me and, truth be
told, you're not delivering on Your end of the bargain. I'm
doing everything I know to do and yet I don't like the way You
are arranging my life."

What's the older brother's biggest problem? It's really
not that difficult to see. Older brothers (or older sisters, for
that part) don't know their true condition—that they live behind a veneer of self-righteousness and they simply have no
way of knowing how bad off they are. Therefore they cannot appreciate God's provision for them. They are clueless to
their condition, they are clueless to God's provision.

And all of that just shows up in this performance-
based, arrogant spirituality. They don't know their heart,
they don't know God's heart, so all they know to do is to
perform, perform, perform. The bottom line is that older

brothers have got to see how much they need to repent of their self-righteousness.

The Pursuing Father

In the parable of the Prodigal Sons, Jesus is teaching us about two ways people try to make their lives work in response to what they believe to be true about God. But both of these ways are equally disastrous. They both sabotage the true knowledge of God. And they fail against the backdrop of the lead character that begins to emerge in this parable. He truly is the loving, pursuing father.

And Jesus presents this father as one unlike any father we've ever known, perhaps unlike any image of God we've carried around in our heart. A father that extends himself, a father that embraces younger brothers and older brothers alike. But you see, here's the irony in the parable: why is it that we only find one of the two brothers responding readily to the affection of such a loving father? Why the younger brother? What is it about younger brothers that makes them respond so much quicker than self-righteous older brothers?

They hit rock bottom sooner. They simply come to the end of themselves. And as they come to the end of themselves, they embrace their brokenness. They are more ready to say, "I am a mess." And in that tragic sense of disconnect, they risk going home. And as they go home, as they make their movement towards what they hope will be life, the father emerges.

How Jesus begins to characterize that father figure—the true God who is in the story! The father, from a far-away place, sees his younger son moving toward him, and the father hikes up his skirt, his gown. He begins to run toward his son. And as the Scripture tells us, he falls on the neck of this younger son and he kisses him: the kisses of God the Father.

Pride and Humility

It's so tragic, so sad to see that this older brother simply has no comprehension that he needs the father's embrace. And yet don't we see the same thing for a while in the story of the younger brother? That's what really ties these two brothers together. They're in the same family, they're smitten with the same disease that we're smitten with. It's called pride.

God knows the proud from afar, but gives grace to the humble. He pursues younger brothers that have wasted their lives, squandered the inheritance. He pursues self-righteous, toxically religious people that still don't get it—that still don't get that it's about a relationship with the living God.

I pray we find ourselves in the stories of these two young men. Perhaps we're a part of each. But all of us need to deal with the fact that it's pride, more than anything else, that keeps us distanced from God. He is pursuing us, He is lavishing on us His affections. Jesus tells this story because He knows the end of the story is His providing the very righteousness we need that we can never find in either religion or irreligion. Only in the gift of God's Son Jesus — who shows us the Father's heart, who invites you and me to think about our pride, our unbelief, our self-righteousness, our despair, our shame — can we really respond to Him who loves us and who is pursuing us. Let's humble ourselves. Let's repent of our unrighteousness, our self-righteousness and receive God's grace.

ADDITIONAL VERSES
FOR STUDY AND REFLECTION

LUKE 18:9-14

To some who were confident of their own righteousness and looked down on everybody else, Jesus told this parable: "Two men went up to the temple to pray, one a Pharisee and the other a tax collector. The Pharisee stood up and prayed about himself: 'God, I thank you that I am not like other men—robbers, evildoers, adulterers—or even like this tax collector. I fast twice a week and give a tenth of all I get.'

"But the tax collector stood at a distance. He would not even look up to heaven, but beat his breast and said, 'God, have mercy on me, a sinner.'

"I tell you that this man, rather than the other, went home justified before God. For everyone who exalts himself will be humbled, and he who humbles himself will be exalted."

*   *   *

MATTHEW 23:1-4; 11-28

Then Jesus said to the crowds and to his disciples: "The teachers of the law and the Pharisees sit in Moses' seat. So you must obey them and do everything they tell you. But do not do what they do, for they do not practice what they preach. They tie up heavy loads and put them on men's shoulders, but they themselves are not willing to lift a finger to move them....

"The greatest among you will be your servant. For whoever exalts himself will be humbled, and whoever humbles himself will be exalted.

"Woe to you, teachers of the law and Pharisees, you hypocrites! You shut the kingdom of heaven in men's faces. You yourselves do not enter, nor will you let those enter who are trying to.

"Woe to you, teachers of the law and Pharisees, you hypocrites! You travel over land and sea to win a single convert, and when he becomes one, you make him twice as much a son of hell as you are.

"Woe to you, blind guides! You say, 'If anyone swears by the temple, it means nothing; but if anyone swears by the gold of the temple, he is bound by his oath.' You blind fools! Which is greater: the gold, or the temple that makes the gold sacred? You also say, 'If anyone swears by the altar, it means nothing; but if anyone swears by the gift on it, he is bound by his oath.' You blind men! Which is greater: the gift, or the altar that makes the gift sacred? Therefore, he who swears by the altar swears by it and by everything on it. And he who swears by the temple swears by it and by the one who dwells in it. And he who swears by heaven swears by God's throne and by the one who sits on it.

"Woe to you, teachers of the law and Pharisees, you hypocrites! You give a tenth of your spices—mint, dill and cummin. But you have neglected the more important matters of the law—justice, mercy and faithfulness. You should have practiced the latter, without neglecting the former. You blind guides! You strain out a gnat but swallow a camel.

"Woe to you, teachers of the law and Pharisees, you hypocrites! You clean the outside of the cup and dish, but inside they are full of greed and self-indulgence. Blind Pharisee! First clean the inside of the cup and dish, and then the outside also will be clean.

"Woe to you, teachers of the law and Pharisees, you hypocrites! You are like whitewashed tombs, which look beautiful on the outside but on the inside are full of dead men's bones and everything unclean. In the same way, on the outside you appear to people as righteous but on the inside you are full of hypocrisy and wickedness."

*　　　　*　　　　*

PROVERBS 29:23

A man's pride brings him low, but a man of lowly spirit gains honor.

*　　　　*　　　　*

JAMES 4:6

But he gives us more grace. That is why Scripture says:
"God opposes the proud but gives grace to the humble."

Epilogue

The friend who attends the bridegroom waits and listens for him, and is full of joy when he hears the bridegroom's voice. That joy is mine, and it is now complete. He must become greater; I must become less.

The one who comes from above is above all; the one who is from the earth belongs to the earth, and speaks as one from the earth. The one who comes from heaven is above all. JOHN 3:29-31

We hope you enjoyed studying these six parables of Jesus. One of the goals of this study was to teach you more about the Kingdom of God and your daily involvement in it. We hope that the film medium was a helpful tool to expanding your understanding of these parables as they relate to the broader Kingdom of God.

It was a privilege for us to be able to work with these rich stories of Jesus. At the end of it all, however, we want to emphasize how unimportant the films are in comparison to what is truly important: the Word of God. We encourage you to continue spending time with the parables and, if interested, to pursue more extensive research and study of the parables on your own.

To help you in that pursuit we have compiled resources on the parables at our website www.modernparable.com.

In closing, thank you for taking time to use this study. We sincerely hope that through it you have grown in your relationship with our Lord Jesus Christ.

- THOMAS PURIFOY, JR. & JONATHAN ROGERS

About the Authors

Thomas Purifoy, Jr. is the producer of *Modern Parables: Living in the Kingdom of God*. He has been a Sunday School teacher for over fifteen years and has had the opportunity to teach a range of ages from adult to kindergarten. He currently lives in Nashville, Tennessee with his wife and three girls. His production company is Compass Cinema which produced the *Modern Parables* films.

Jonathan Rogers, Ph.D. is an author and editor living in Nashville, Tennessee. He is best known for his Wilderking series of adventure novels for young readers. More information can be found at www.wilderking.com.

LaVergne, TN USA
15 January 2011
212612LV00004B/2/P